CW01221233

THE BISMARCK CHASE

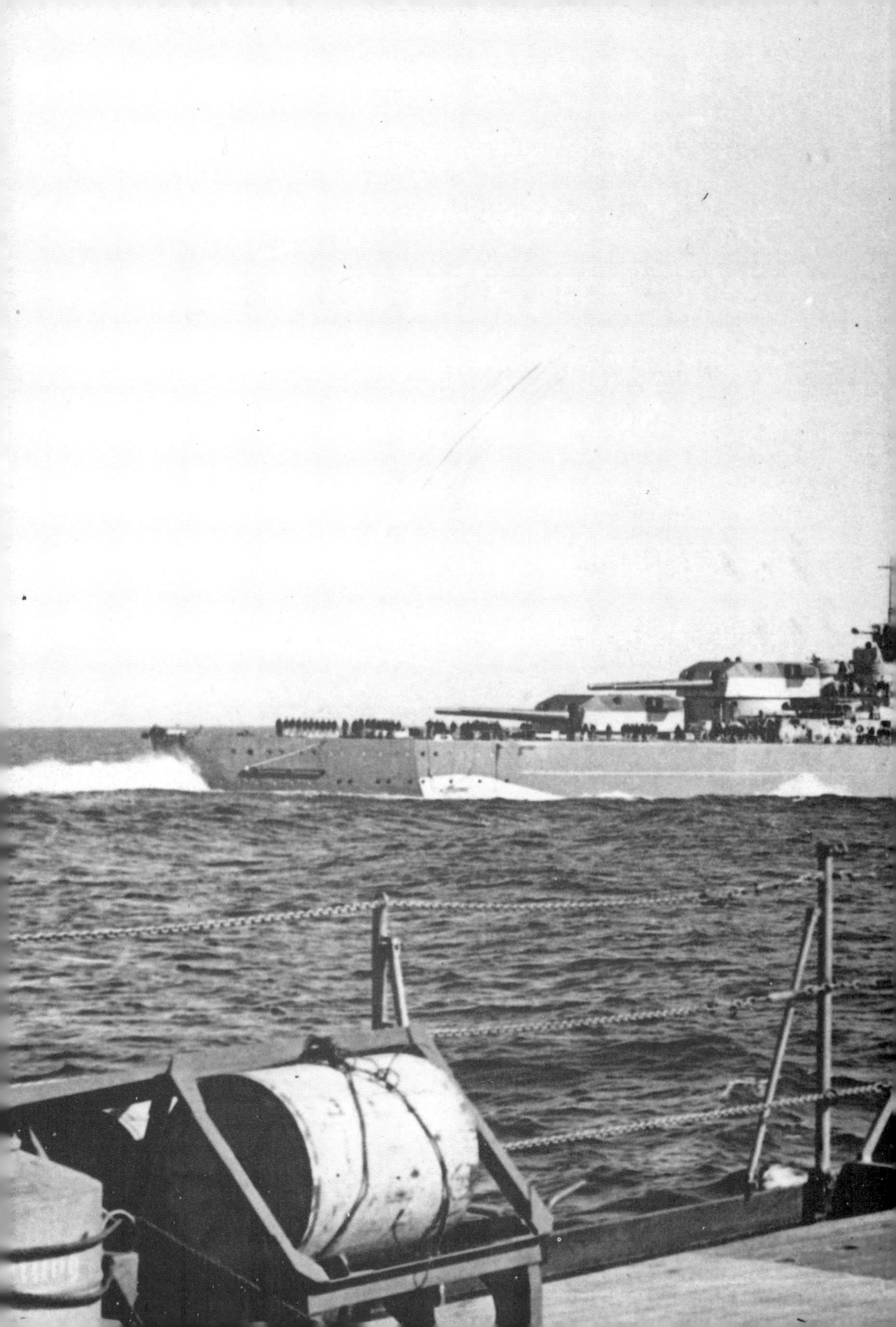

THE BISMARCK CHASE

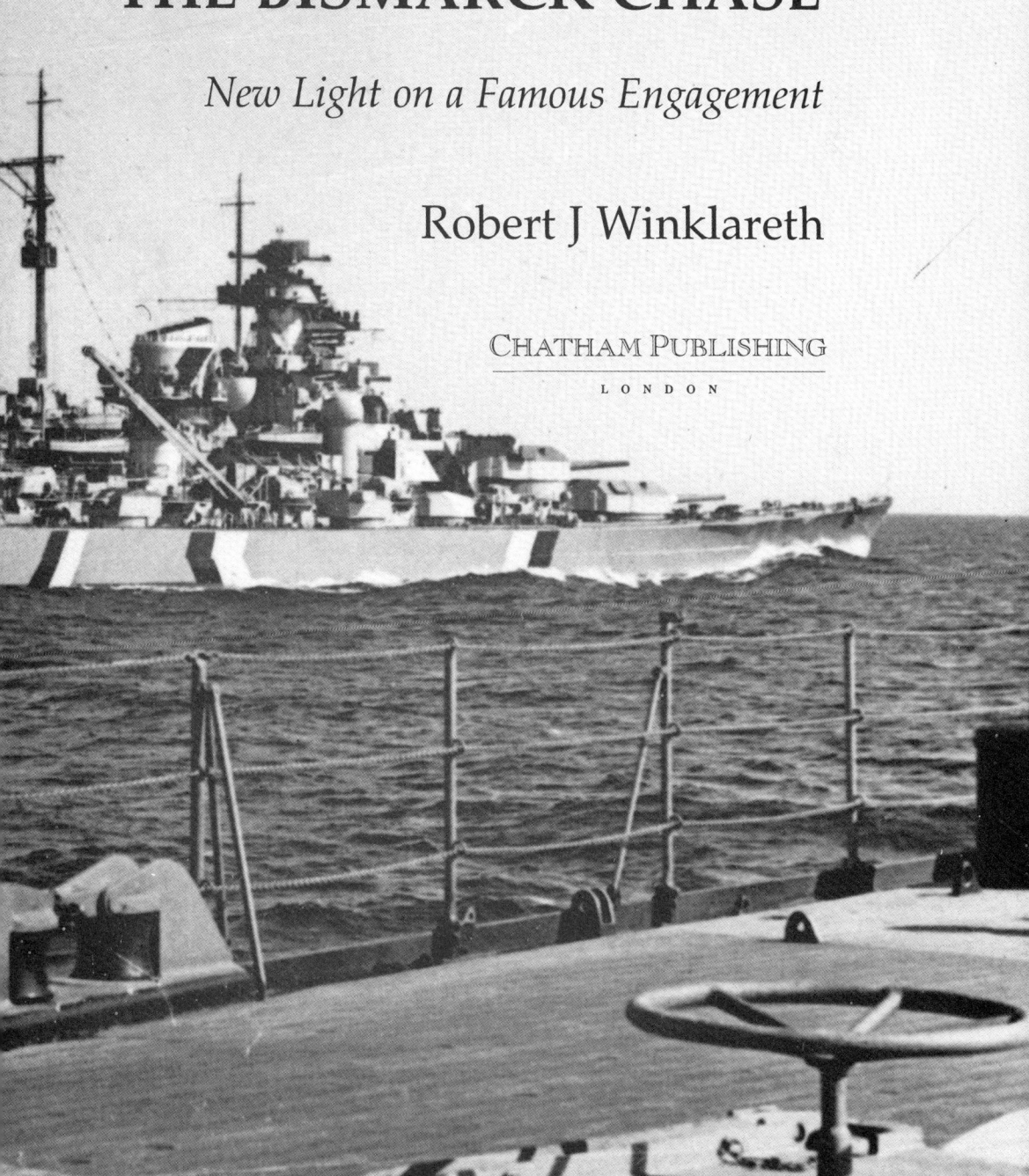

New Light on a Famous Engagement

Robert J Winklareth

CHATHAM PUBLISHING
LONDON

Dedication

This book is dedicated to the memory of my eldest son, Franklin, who shared my interest in history.

Frontispiece: *Bismarck* en route to Norway, 20 May 1941, at the beginning of her first and only sortie, photographed from *Prinz Eugen*. (Imperial War Museum: HU374)

Copyright © Robert J Winklareth 1998

First published in Great Britain in 1998 by Chatham Publishing,
61 Frith Street, London W1V 5TA

Chatham Publishing is an imprint of Gerald Duckworth & Co Ltd

British Library Cataloguing in Publication Data
A catalogue record for this book is available from the
British Library

ISBN 1 86176 076 0

All rights reserved. No part of this publication may be reproduced or transmitted in any form or by any means, electronic or mechanical, including photocopying, recording, or any information storage and retrieval system, without either prior permission in writing from the publisher or a licence permitting restricted copying. The right of Robert J Winklareth to be identified as the author of this work has been asserted by him in accordance with the Copyright, Designs and Patents Act 1988.

All maps and pencil sketches drawn by the author.

Typeset by Dorwyn Ltd, Rowlands Castle, Hants

Printed and bound in Great Britain by Bookcraft (Bath) Ltd

Contents

Acknowledgements   6
Preface   7

1   The Dreadnought Era – the Genesis of HMS *Hood*   9
2   The New Generation – *King George V* and *Prince of Wales*   26
3   The Rebirth of German Seapower – *Bismarck*   37
4   *Bismarck* Becomes Operational   45
5   The British Response   57
6   Initial Contact   68
7   Enemy in Sight   76
8   Open Fire   84
9   The Loss of HMS *Hood*   91
10   HMS *Prince of Wales* Fights Alone   102
11   *Bismarck* Escapes   117
12   *Bismarck* is Discovered   128
13   The *Bismarck* is Disabled   135
14   The Final Battle   150
15   Epilogue   164

Appendix A: Naval Gunnery   173
Appendix B: Bibliography   183
Index   185

Acknowledgements

First, I would like to acknowledge the work of the many authors of books and articles previously written on this subject. Their work provided the general public with a good overall understanding of what transpired prior to, during, and after the famous battle between the battleship *Bismarck* and the Royal Navy.

In addition, I wish to thank the following people who provided information and clarification for some of the material contained in this book:

- Ms Nina F Lande, Information Office, Bergen, Norway.

- Mr Arnór Sigurjónsson, Embassy of Iceland, Washington.

- Mr Thorbjörn Jónsson, Foreign Affairs Ministry, Iceland.

- Hauptmann Hippchen, Military History Information Office, Potsdam, Germany.

The author is also deeply indebted to Prof. Dr. Jürgen Rohwer, noted naval historian and former Director of the Library for Contemporary History in Stuttgart, Germany, for his constructive review of this work and his enthusiastic support for its publication.

Preface

At dawn on 24 May 1941, a British naval force consisting of the battlecruiser *Hood*, battleship *Prince of Wales,* and two heavy cruisers brought to bay the German battleship *Bismarck* and her heavy cruiser consort *Prinz Eugen* in the waters of the North Atlantic off the coast of Greenland. Although the *Hood* was lost in this initial engagement, the damage inflicted on the *Bismarck* forced her to abandon her primary mission of raiding Allied convoys and to head for the French coast for repairs. This placed her in the path of other British forces converging on the German flagship and eventually led to her destruction three days later.

Many books and articles have been written on the subject, some by famous authors, some by participants on both sides, and others by noted naval historians. With the wealth of information already available, there seemed little more that could be added to that famous saga. A careful review of those earlier accounts, however, reveals that some inconsistencies exist in what has been previously written and indicates that some aspects of the story require further clarification. This book is an attempt to fill in some of the gaps and help set the record straight.

This book is based on a comprehensive analysis of the generally accepted facts concerning the battle between the British and German forces off the coast of Greenland and the subsequent destruction of the *Bismarck*. It portrays the most probable sequence of events that can be derived from a detailed study of the information and photographic material available. It resolves some of the inconsistencies contained in previous works, such as the course of the *Bismarck* and *Prinz Eugen* in relation to that of the British force. By establishing the likely track of the German squadron, a clearer insight can be obtained regarding the moves and countermoves undertaken by each side and a better understanding can be achieved as to how the battle was waged by the respective commanders.

It also provides an explanation as to why the gunners on HMS *Hood* could have mistaken the *Prinz Eugen* for the *Bismarck* and caused the wrong ship to be fired upon at the beginning of the battle, and corrects the orientation of several photographs taken of the *Bismarck* from the *Prinz Eugen* that have been printed in reverse in many previous publications. The proper interpretation of those photographs in their true perspective contributes greatly to an appreciation of what actually occurred during the battle.

The primary purpose of this book is to tell the story of what happened in clear and easy-to-understand terms. It concentrates mainly on the battle involving the *Hood* and *Prince of Wales* versus the *Bismarck* and *Prinz Eugen* on 24 May, but it also provides a broad scope of related information ranging from the genesis of HMS *Hood* during the First World War to the discovery of the wreck of the *Bismarck* on the ocean floor in 1989. This book is intended to be a stand-alone document, but it also supplements the works that have already been written on this subject and which do not fully cover the specific areas addressed herein.

Appendix A provides general background information on naval gunnery for a better understanding of the technical problems associated with naval combat. This information is consolidated into an appendix rather than being inserted at each appropriate point to avoid cluttering the text and interrupting the flow of the story. Appendix B contains a bibliography of some of the previous works published on this subject.

Robert J Winklareth
January 1998

CHAPTER 1

The Dreadnought Era – The Genesis of HMS *Hood*

The British battlecruiser *Hood* was the culmination of the 'Dreadnought' era of warship design and construction during the period just prior to and during the First World War. Conceived at the beginning of the twentieth century as the first 'all-big-gun' battleship, HMS *Dreadnought* revolutionised naval architecture throughout the world by replacing guns of various different calibres, as traditionally used on capital ships of most nations, into a single calibre for the main armament of the ship. The *Dreadnought*, a ship of 17,900 tons, carried ten 12in guns in five twin turrets, three along the centreline of the ship and two wing turrets on either side of the ship adjacent to the foremast.

The British all-big-gun concept was the brainchild of Admiral Sir John Fisher, who as First Sea Lord presented his views to the Cabinet in 1904. The Japanese victory over the Russian fleet in the Strait of Tsushima in the following year tended to support the concept, confirming the greater damage potential of heavy guns. With the increased accuracy of the latest design 12in guns and improved fire control systems, it was now possible to fire broadsides of eight or more 12in guns at longer ranges with increased possibility of hits.

Earlier battleships usually had two turrets, one forward and one aft, each mounting two 12in or comparable heavy-calibre guns with an array of smaller-calibre guns mounted along the sides of the ship. Salvoes fired with only four heavy-calibre guns had far less chance of hitting the target at long range than those from twice that many guns. Smaller-calibre weapons had only a remote chance of scoring a hit at longer ranges, and the splashes of their shells often

1-1 HMS *Dreadnought*, the first 'all-big-gun' battleship, in 1907. (Imperial War Museum: Q21183)

interfered with the sighting of shell splashes from the main armament. In addition to these considerations, the use of guns of a single calibre also had logistical advantages, allowing the use of standard ammunition, spare gun tubes and parts.

The *Dreadnought* was completed in 1906, and other countries soon followed suit with their own versions of the Dreadnought design concept. In the armaments race that preceded the First World War, Dreadnoughts of all countries progressively increased in size and in the calibre of guns they carried. The British continued to be the most prolific in their construction, but the German Kaiser did his best to try to keep up with his rival. The United States, France, Italy, Russia, Austria-Hungary, and Japan also participated in the prestigious naval armaments race. In fact, the United States had initiated an all-big-gun battleship design earlier than the British, but they did not complete their first two Dreadnoughts until 1910.

In addition to Dreadnought battleships, Great Britain, Germany, and Japan also undertook the construction of a number of battlecruisers. The British battlecruiser, also a brainchild of Admiral Fisher, was conceived as a cross between a battleship and a cruiser, combining the firepower of the former with the speed of the latter. However, to achieve this speed, battlecruisers had to be less heavily-armoured than the battleships, and generally carried fewer heavy guns. Their speed was also enhanced by a hull design that gave them a greater length to beam ratio than battleships. The size of battlecruisers approached that of battleships, but they were usually somewhat longer.

Great Britain built nine more battleships with the same armament as the *Dreadnought* (ten 12in guns). Superfiring turrets were first introduced into the Royal Navy with the battleship *Neptune*, which entered service in 1911. This ships had one twin 12in gun turret superimposed over another at the stern of the ship. In addition, six battlecruisers with eight 12in guns were also built between 1908 and 1911, three of the *Invincible* class and three of the *Indefatigable* class. These were the last capital ships to mount 12in guns as the trend toward larger vessels and more powerful armament continued.

In 1909, Great Britain laid down the first battleships (*Orion* class) and battlecruisers (*Lion* class) with 13.5in guns. While 12in guns had been mounted in wing turrets along the sides of a ship, the heavier 13.5in guns were all mounted in turrets on the centreline for greater stability. By the onset of the First World War in August 1914, twelve battleships mounting ten 13.5in guns and four battlecruisers with eight 13.5in guns had been completed.

In 1912, a newly-developed 15in gun was adopted as the standard for the Royal Navy in new capital ship construction. A new breed of battleship was then planned, not only carry this weapon but also to achieve a significant increase in speed. In October 1912, the British laid down the *Queen Elizabeth*, the first of five battleships of that class. The *Queen Elizabeth* class displaced 29,150 tons, were

600ft long, and had a beam of 90ft and a draught of 30ft. With four Parsons steam turbine engines generating 75,000 horsepower, they had a design speed of 25 knots, thereby heralding the new concept of the 'fast battleship'. Increased space requirements for the more powerful machinery needed to achieve this greater speed necessitated the elimination of midships turrets. These ships were therefore of a more compact design, mounting four twin turrets, two forward and two aft, with one turret superimposed over the other turret at each end. The eight 15in guns mounted on these battleships would actually give them an increased broadside weight over the ten 13.5in guns used on earlier battleships (7.5 tons versus 7.0 tons).

1–2 HMS *Warspite* (right) and *Malaya* (left) of the *Queen Elizabeth* class, armed with eight 15in guns, in 1916. (Imperial War Museum: SP1487)

The *Queen Elizabeth* class was followed a year later by the *Royal Sovereign* class, also consisting of five ships mounting the same armament. These ships displaced 28,000 tons, were 580ft long, and had a beam of 88ft and draught of 30ft. The *Royal Sovereign* class battleships were a little smaller and had a speed of only 21 knots compared with the nominal 25 knots for the *Queen Elizabeth*s, but otherwise, the two classes were generally comparable. All ten ships of these two classes were retained by Great Britain after 1918, and they continued to serve as the backbone of the Royal Navy during the Second World War.

Two battlecruisers with the new 15in guns were also built, the 26,500-ton *Renown* and *Repulse*, both launched in 1916. These ships were nearly 800ft long and had a beam of 90ft and a draught of 26ft. They carried six 15in guns in three twin turrets, two superfiring forward and one aft, and had a speed of 31 knots, considerably faster than contemporary battleships. These two ships also went on to serve with distinction during the Second World War.

At the outbreak of the First World War, the Royal Navy appropriated three battleships that were being built by British private shipyards for other countries. These included the *Agincourt*, a large vessel mounting fourteen 12in guns in seven twin turrets, the largest number of heavy guns ever carried by a Dreadnought battleship, which was being built for Turkey by Armstrong at Elswick on the River Tyne. The battleship *Reshadieh*, with the standard British armament of ten 13.5in guns, was also being built for Turkey at the Vickers shipyard located at Barrow-in-Furness, and was taken into the Royal Navy as HMS *Erin*. Armstrong was also building a battleship for Chile that mounted ten 14in guns of a new design. That ship was completed for the Royal Navy in 1915 as the *Canada*.

At the turn of the century, the main armament of German battleships had increased in calibre from 9.4in to 11in. In 1908, this was further increased to 12in to match the British Dreadnoughts, but some ships continued to be built with the earlier 11in gun. When the Germans realised that the British would be adopting the 15in gun, they decided to follow suit. In 1913, they laid down the battleship *Bayern*, one of four ships planned to answer the British threat.

The *Bayern* class ships would displace 28,000 tons, be 560ft long, and have a beam of 99ft and draught of 28ft. They would have a speed of 22 knots and carry the same armament as the new British battleships, *ie*, eight 15in guns in four twin turrets, two forward and two aft. Only the *Bayern* and her sister ship, the *Baden*, were ever completed and entered service. Since these were the last German capital ships completed, their design was the best available when Germany began planning for the *Bismarck* class battleships in the late 1930s.

The United States actually drew up the first design for an 'all-big-gun' battleship with the *South Carolina* class, but the construction of these ships was delayed by several years. The two ships of this class, *South Carolina* and *Michigan*, were not completed until 1910, four years after HMS *Dreadnought*, and they therefore lost the distinction of being the first all-big-gun battleships to enter service. These ships displaced 16,000 tons, carried eight 12in guns, and had a speed of 18.5 knots. Their guns were arranged in four turrets, two forward and two aft, with one turret superfiring over the other turret at each end of the ship, making them the first capital ships to use superfiring turrets.

The United States built six more Dreadnoughts between 1909 and 1914, the four ships of the *Delaware* and *Florida* classes with ten 12in guns and the two *Wyoming* class ships mounting twelve 12in guns in six twin turrets. By 1914, the US Navy had increased the calibre of its guns to 14in with the 27,000-ton battleships *New York* and *Texas*, each of which carried ten of these guns in five twin turrets, two forward and three aft. In 1916, these ships were followed by two slightly larger battleships of the *Nevada* class that also carried ten 14in guns, but in only four turrets. The two lower turrets, both forward and aft, were triple turrets while the two superior turrets at each end of the ship carried two guns. This was the first use of triple turrets in American capital ships. They then built seven ships of about 33,000 tons displacement with twelve 14in guns in four triple turrets, two forward and two aft.

The last three American battleships of First World War vintage to be constructed were laid down in 1917. These ships of the *Colorado* class were similar to the preceding seven battleships, but carried

The Dreadnought Era

1–3 The battlecruiser HMS *Inflexible* in 1908. (Imperial War Museum: Q39246)

eight 16in guns in twin turrets, with two turrets superfiring fore and aft.

France joined the Dreadnought race late, and it was not until 1910 that four ships of the *Courbet* class, each displacing 23,500 tons and carrying twelve 12in guns were ordered. These ships were then followed in 1912 by three more battleships of the *Bretagne* class, each of which carried ten 13.4in guns. Italy embarked on a similar programme, laying down the 20,500-ton *Dante Alighieri* with twelve 12in guns in 1909. She was the first capital ship in service with triple turrets, and all twelve guns were so mounted in four centreline turrets. In the next three years, Italy built five more battleships with thirteen 12in guns in five mounts, three of which were triple

1–4 HMS *Hood*, the largest warship in the world, on her sea trials in 1920, when she made a top speed of 32 knots. (Imperial War Museum: Q17879)

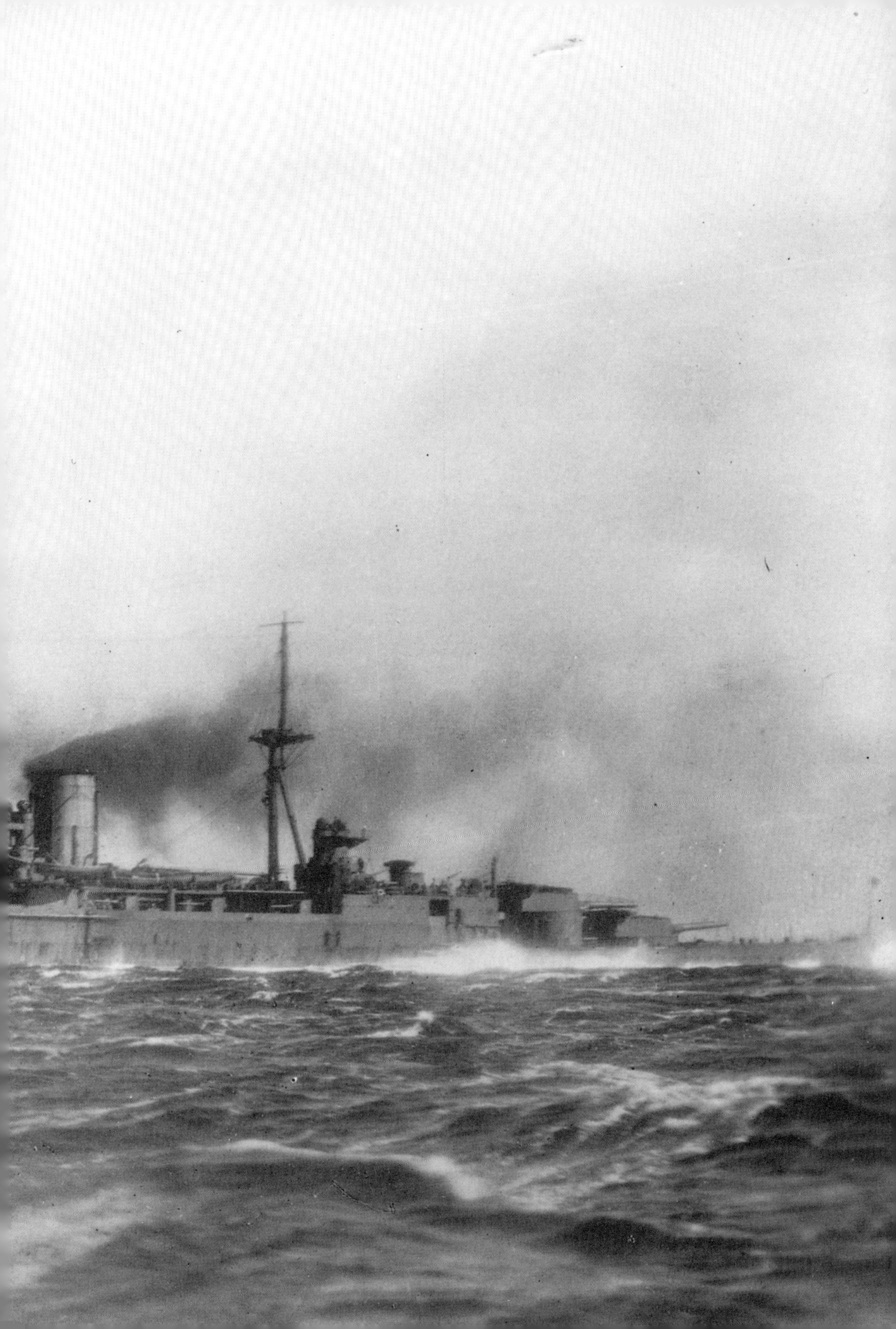

mounts at deck level and two twin mounts superfiring over the triple mounts fore and aft.

Not to be outdone by the major European powers and the United States, the emerging naval power of Japan also began a Dreadnought construction programme in 1910 with two 30,000-ton battleships *Fuso* and *Yamashiro* carrying twelve 12in guns. In 1911, Japan laid down three 27,500-ton battlecruisers which were later to be rebuilt as 'fast battleships'. These ships were based on the *Kongo*, the British Vickers-built prototype, and they were equipped with eight 14in guns. These were followed by the battleships *Ise* and *Hyuga* mounting twelve 14in guns in six twin turrets. In 1917, they laid down two of the first Dreadnoughts to mount 16in guns, the 32,700-ton *Nagato* and *Mutsu*, each of which carried eight of those guns in four twin turrets. These ships were very fast, with *Nagato* reportedly making over 26 knots on her sea trials, continuing the trend toward 'high-speed battleships', although her speed was a well-kept secret for most of the inter-war years.

Several other countries undertook limited Dreadnought construction programmes. Imperial Russia laid down four 23,000-ton battleships of the *Gangut* class in 1909 and three more of the *Imperatritsa Mariya* class in 1911, all with twelve 12in guns in four triple mounts at deck level along the centreline of the ship. Austria-Hungary built the four 20,000-ton *Tegetthoff* class battleships carrying twelve 12in guns in four triple turrets beginning in 1910. Spain's three battleships of the *Espana* class, laid down beginning in 1909, were the smallest Dreadnoughts ever built at only 15,700 tons. They mounted eight 12in guns in four twin turrets. Other countries seeking to join the Dreadnought race but lacking the capability to build their own, such as Turkey and the nations of South America, bought their battleships from the shipyards of the major powers.

During the early years of the First World War, the British Admiralty developed the concept of the ultimate capital ship, one that would incorporate the best features of a battleship and a battlecruiser. The ship would have the same armament and armour protection as the latest battleships, but it would also be able to steam at a speed of over 30 knots, comparable to that of the latest battlecruisers. To achieve all of these characteristics, the ship would have to be considerably larger, and in particular longer, than any of the current British capital ships. Contracts were awarded to build three of these ships: the *Hood* went to John Brown, the *Howe* went to Cammell Laird, and the *Rodney* went to Fairfield. A fourth ship, the *Anson*, was later ordered from Armstrong.

The new class took its name from a family with a rich tradition in the Royal Navy, beginning with Samuel, Viscount Hood (1724-1816). After a distinguished naval career involving service in North America and the West Indies, and later in the Mediterranean, he was named Viscount Hood of Whitley. Samuel's younger brother, Alexander (1726-1814), also had a successful career in the Royal Navy, attaining the rank of vice-admiral while in service. He became Lord Bridport in 1794, and in 1800 was elevated to a viscountcy. A cousin with the same name, Sir Samuel Hood (1762-1814), distinguished himself in action in the Mediterranean and subsequently became the Commander of the East Indies Fleet as a vice-admiral. A brother of Sir Samuel Hood with the same name as his cousin, Alexander Hood (1758-1798), was killed while commanding the 74-gun *Mars* in its successful fight against the French *Hercule* of the same rate. The death at Jutland in 1916 of Rear-Admiral Horace Hood, another member of that family, may also have influenced the naming of the ship.

HMS *Hood*, the third British warship that would bear that illustrious name, was laid down at the end of May 1916, just as the Battle of Jutland was raging in the North Sea. As designed, she would displace 36,000 tons (later increased to 41,200 tons) and have an overall length of just over 860ft (more than 200ft longer than the battleships of her day), a beam of 105ft, and a draught of 32ft. Her turbines would generate 150,000 shaft horsepower and drive her through four shafts at a sustained speed of 31 knots. The new super-battlecruiser would carry eight 15in guns in four twin turrets, the same as contemporary British battleships, and twelve 5.5in guns in single mounts.

During the Battle of Jutland (31 May-1 June 1916), three British battlecruisers were destroyed when German shells plunged through their relatively thinly armoured decks and exploded in

The Bismarck Chase

1–5 The destruction of the battlecruiser HMS *Invincible* at the Battle of Jutland, 31 May 1916, showing her centre magazines exploding. (Imperial War Museum: SP2468)

their magazines. The *Indefatigable*, a ship of 18,500 tons armed with eight 12in guns, was the first to be hit. She was part of Admiral Beatty's Battlecruiser Force when she was hit by a salvo from the German battlecruiser *Von Der Tann*, and went down with only two survivors out of a crew of over 1000 officers and men. The next to be hit was the *Queen Mary*, a newer ship of the *Lion* class displacing 26,300 tons and carrying eight 13.5in guns. Also part of the Battlecruiser Force, she sank with the loss of over 1200 lives.

The third battlecruiser to be lost at Jutland was the *Invincible*, flagship of the 3rd Battlecruiser Squadron attached to Admiral Jellicoe's Battle Fleet. She displaced 17,300 tons and carried eight 12in guns in four twin turrets, one forward, one aft, and two wing turrets at the centre of the ship. Under concentrated enemy fire, she was hit amidships by a shell that caused the magazines of her centre wing turrets to detonate. She broke in half and sank with a loss of all but five of her complement of nearly 800 officers and men. Among those lost with the *Invincible* was the Commander of the 3rd Battlecruiser Squadron, Rear-Admiral Horace Hood.

The experience of Jutland led to technical improvements being incorporated into the *Hood* while she was still building. This included a significant increase in the horizontal deck armour over her magazines and engine spaces and increased armour protection for her turrets. Her gun mounts were also redesigned to allow for an increase in the maximum elevation of her guns from 20° to 30°, to allow for longer-range fire. *Hood* was launched in August 1918, but was not completed until early 1920, more than a year after the end of the First World War. She attained a speed of 32 knots during her sea trials, and was commissioned in May 1920. Work on her three sister-ships had been suspended in 1917, leaving the *Hood* as the only British super-battlecruiser to emerge from the First World War.

Under the Washington Naval Treaty of 1922, the displacement of new capital ships was limited to 35,000 tons. Although the *Hood* exceeded that limit, Great Britain was permitted to retain that ship as an exception to the general rule. In all, Great Britain was allowed to retain fifteen capital ships, and the Admiralty chose the five battleships of the *Queen Elizabeth* class, five battleships of the *Royal Sovereign* class, and two post-war battleships, the *Nelson* and *Rodney*. Besides the *Hood*, two smaller battlecruisers, the *Renown* and *Repulse*, were also retained. Another provision of the Washington Naval Treaty allowed for the eventual replacement of these capital ships, but only after each ship had been in service for over 20 years. Ironically, under this provision, the *Hood* would have become eligible for replacement in 1941, the very year in which she met her fate.

During the inter-war years, *Hood* was the pride of the Royal Navy, and in addition to serving as the flagship of the Home Fleet, she was employed in 'showing the flag' at trouble spots and for ceremonial functions throughout the British Empire. She represented British interests in every corner of the world, and served in the international neutrality patrol in Spanish waters during the Spanish Civil War (1936-38). In May 1937, the *Hood* participated in the naval review at Spithead to celebrate the coronation of King George VI. Until the advent of new 35,000-ton battleships in the late 1930s, the she was considered to be the most powerful battleship in the world.

From 1922 to 1939, various programmes were undertaken by the Royal Navy to modernise their capital ships. One by one, they were brought into the Royal Dockyards to be upgraded, often involving an extensive reconstruction of the ship to incorporate all of the necessary improvements. The Washington Naval Treaty allowed the major naval powers to increase the displacement of their capital ships by up to 3000 tons for the purpose of improving protection against torpedoes and aerial bombs. Great Britain took advantage of this provision to increase the thickness of the deck armour and adding anti-torpedo bulges along the sides of most of their capital ships. Other improvements included the addition of a High-Angle Control System (HACS) incorporating medium-calibre anti-aircraft guns and their fire control directors.

In 1927, consideration was given to increasing the horizontal deck armour over the magazines and engine compartments of the *Hood*. This proposal was rejected at the time because it could not be accomplished without a major reconstruction of the ship. She was already lying deep in the water as a result of earlier modifications, and therefore her buoyancy would have to be increased to accommodate the weight of any additional armour. Being among the last capital ships to be built before the moratorium on warship construction was instituted, the *Hood* had a greater degree of armour protection than some of the older capital ships retained by Great Britain, and therefore her reconstruction was given low priority.

Hood was finally scheduled for a full reconstruction in 1939, particularly to increase her deck armour and to make other essential improvements. In view of the threat of war at that time, the Admiralty decided not to lay her up for such extensive work, carrying out only minor modifications such as replacing her single-mount 4in AA guns with four twin mounts. Critically, this meant that she never received the increased deck armour she needed.

When her refit was completed at Portsmouth Royal Dockyard in August 1939, the *Hood* sailed north to rejoin the Home Fleet at its base at Scapa Flow at the northern tip of Scotland just in time for the outbreak of the Second World War. Germany invaded Poland on 1 September, and two days later, Britain and France declared war on Germany. The *Hood* was already at sea on patrol when the war broke out. In late September, she came under a bombing attack by German aircraft in the North Sea, but received only a glancing hit that did little damage.

The *Hood* was continuously on the alert to counter German naval activity in the North Sea area, and she was subsequently assigned to convoy duty in the North Atlantic. In the spring of 1940, she was sent to Devonport Royal Dockyard for a further refit. At that time, her remaining 5.5in guns were replaced by three more twin 4in anti-aircraft gun mounts, bringing her total up to seven, and additional improvements were made to her secondary armament fire control system. These modification, together with earlier refits, brought her standard displacement up to a little over 45,000 tons and reduced her maximum speed to just under 30 knots.

On 1 July, Force H was formed in the Mediterranean with the *Hood* as its flagship, and including the battleships *Resolution* and *Valiant*, aircraft carrier *Ark Royal*, cruisers *Arethusa* and *Enterprise*, and eleven destroyers. No sooner had Force H been formed then it was called into action, not against the Germans, but against Britain's former ally. France had fallen to the Germans on 17 June 1940, and it was vital that her powerful fleet not fall into German hands. Force H sailed from Gibraltar to Oran on the northern coast of Algeria to blockade the French naval base at Mers-el-Kebir. When the French failed to respond to several alternatives for neutralising their naval forces, the British felt compelled to take direct action.

Shortly before 1800hrs on 3 July, the *Hood*, together with the battleships *Resolution* and *Valiant*, opened fire on French naval units in the harbour at a range of 18,000 yards. The old battleship *Bretagne* was soon hit and set on fire. She quickly sank with the loss of over 800 men. The equally elderly battleship *Provence* was severely damaged and had to be beached. The new 26,500-ton battleship *Dunkerque* was also heavily damaged and rendered inoperative. Her sister-ship, the *Strasbourg*, was able to raise steam and escape

1–6 HMS *Hood* in port on 21 August 1940, after her final refit. Note the Unrotated Projectile launcher, covered by a tarpaulin, to the right of the second funnel. (Imperial War Museum: A180)

from the harbour through the smoke of battle. Attempts by aircraft from the *Ark Royal* to bomb and torpedo the *Strasbourg* failed, and she made it safely to the port of Toulon on the southern coast of France.

In August 1940, the *Hood* returned to Scapa Flow where she participated in several missions to intercept German warships on raiding forays in the North Sea and North Atlantic. She underwent

The Dreadnought Era

another refit at Rosyth during the winter, and then she was sent on patrol off Brest. This was followed by patrols and convoy duty in Icelandic waters. She returned to her home base again early in May 1941 to participate in an exercise with other British warships. That exercise was cut short when word was received that the German battleship *Bismarck* had been spotted in a fjord near Bergen, Norway. The entire Home Fleet had been put on alert to await further orders from the Admiralty concerning this new threat.

As a precautionary measure, the *Hood*, together with the new battleship *Prince of Wales* and six destroyers, were ordered to Iceland in anticipation that the *Bismarck* might use either of the two passages around that island to break out into the North Atlantic. Shortly before midnight on 21 May 1941, the *Hood* sailed from Scapa Flow with over 1420 officers and men aboard under the command of Captain Ralph Kerr. The task force was under the overall command of Rear-Admiral Lancelot E Holland, who flew his flag in the *Hood*.

CHAPTER 2

The New Generation – King George V and Prince of Wales

At the end of the First World War, a concerted disarmament programme was undertaken by the major naval powers to reduce the size of their fleets and to establish a limit on their size for the foreseeable future. Although there was no longer a specific threat to contend with, the naval powers had been anxious to upgrade their fleets with replacement vessels incorporating the latest technological advances as well as taking advantage of lessons learned during the war. The Washington Naval Conference, which was concluded in February 1922, resulted in an agreement to scrap many existing warships and to severely curtail the construction of new vessels. This made economic sense since the major powers were ill-prepared to pursue another naval armaments race.

It was agreed that the capital ships retained by the major naval powers would be limited to a ratio of 5:5:3:1.67:1.67 for Great Britain, the United States, Japan, France and Italy, respectively. When these ratios were translated into the displacement of individual ships that could be retained, the total allocated to each nation amounted to 558,950 tons for Great Britain, 525,850 tons for the United States, 301,320 tons for Japan, 221,170 tons for France, and 182,800 tons for Italy. Recognising the new threat of the torpedo and aerial bomb, the conference agreed that ships retained could be upgraded by the application of anti-torpedo bulges and the installation of thicker deck armour. Such modifications could be made only to the extent that they did not increase the displacement of each ship by more than 3000 tons.

Further limits were imposed on the total displacement of replacement ships as follows: 525,000 tons for Great Britain, 525,000 tons for the United States, 315,000 tons for Japan, 175,000 tons for France, and 175,000 tons for Italy. Retained ships could be replaced only after they exceeded 20 years of age. New capital ships were limited to 35,000 tons displacement and their main armament could not exceed 16in calibre. No new capital ships could be built for 10 years, with the exception of two new ships for Great Britain as replacements for older battleships to compensate for the advanced age of its fleet.

Similar limitations were placed on the total displacement of aircraft carriers that could be maintained by each nation as follows: 135,000 tons each for Great Britain and the United States, 81,000 tons for Japan, and 60,000 tons each for France and Italy. The size of aircraft carriers was limited to 27,000 tons, but each nation could have two carriers of up to 33,000 tons displacement using capital ships already built or under construction that would otherwise have to be scrapped under the terms of the treaty. This allowed Great Britain, the United States and Japan to convert or complete two battleships or battlecruisers as aircraft carriers, which the United States and Japan took full advantage of. Even with this exception, however, the total displacement limitation for each nation would still be applicable.

At the end of the First World War, Great Britain, the United States, and Japan all had large battlecruiser projects that had to be curtailed as a result of the Washington Naval Treaty. In 1921, Great Britain placed orders for four new battlecruisers of the 'G3' design, which were intended to follow the *Hood*. These ships were to displace over 48,000 tons and carry nine 16in guns in three triple turrets. With a 35,000-ton limit for new capital ship construction anticipated in the forthcoming naval conferences, the British Admiralty began to plan for capital ships that would meet this. Beginning with the 'G3' battlecruiser design, naval architects scaled down the size of those ships to come up with the design for a 35,000-ton battleship that would still carry the same armament.

Under the terms of the Treaty, Great Britain was allowed to keep the *Hood* as an exception to the 35,000-ton limit on capital ships, but she could not really politically justify any more ships over that limit. Britain was also allowed to build two new capital ships as replacements for older ships in the fleet, and since 45,000 tons was

2–1 The battleship HMS *Rodney* in 1939, with nine 16in guns in three triple turrets forward. (Imperial War Museum: AFJ3)

considered to be the minimum size for a suitable battlecruiser, she opted for two new battleships based on a scaled-down version of the 'G3' design. This resulted in the construction of the truncated *Nelson* and *Rodney*, with the unusual arrangement of their main armament of nine 16in guns concentrated in three triple turrets, all located forward of the bridge. The compact design of these ships allowed for the consolidation of their magazines in one area where they could be better protected collectively. The 'G3' battlecruiser programme was thereupon cancelled.

The United States did not complete any battlecruisers during the Dreadnought era, but six ships of the *Lexington* class were laid down in 1920-21. Two of those ships, the *Lexington* and *Saratoga*, were ultimately converted into aircraft carriers under the terms of the Washington Naval Treaty, but the remaining four were cancelled. Both the *Lexington* and *Saratoga* displaced 33,000 tons, which corresponded to the agreed-upon limit for two aircraft carriers as an exception to the 27,000-ton general limit. Japan also took advantage of this exception by converting the battleship *Kaga* and battlecruiser *Akagi* into 28,000-ton aircraft carriers.

The London Naval Conference of 1930 extended the moratorium on capital ship construction for five more years, to the end of 1936. Existing capital ships would still be limited to 35,000 tons, but further reduced in number to fifteen each for Great Britain and the United States and nine for Japan. France and Italy refused to sign the agreement and therefore were not included in any specific numerical limitation. The powers agreed to reconvene in 1935 to reconsider the situation, but in the meanwhile, only modernisation of their existing ships could be undertaken.

Before the next London Conference could take place, the secondary naval powers (France, Italy, and Germany) began capital ship building programmes that would soon eclipse that of the Royal Navy. As a response to the German *Panzerschiffe* (see Chapter 3), France laid down the sleek and modern fast battleships *Dunkerque* and *Strasbourg* in 1931 and 1934, respectively, displacing 26,500 tons, armed with eight 13in guns in two quadruple mounts forward, and with a speed of almost 30 knots. Germany had by then effectively renounced the Versailles Treaty, and in 1934, she began building the fast battleships *Gneisenau* and *Scharnhorst*. These ships displaced 32,000 tons, carried nine 11in guns, and had a speed of over 30 knots. These French and German battleships were often referred to as battlecruisers in view of their smaller size, lighter armament, and greater speed than contemporary battleships.

Next came the new generation of '35,000-ton' battleships. They were the first full-scale battleships built since 1922, and they generally exceeded the 35,000-ton limitation as improvements were incorporated into them during final design and construction. In 1934, Italy laid down the first three battleships of the *Littorio* class, which carried nine 15in guns in three triple mounts and had a speed of 30 knots. France countered with the *Richelieu* in 1935 and *Jean Bart*, in 1936. These ships displaced 35,000 tons and carried eight 15in guns in two quadruple turrets, both forward of the bridge structure as with the *Dunkerque* class. Based on the separate Anglo-German Naval Treaty of 1935, Germany laid down the *Bismarck* and *Tirpitz* in 1936. These ships were to carry eight 15in guns in four twin turrets, two forward and two aft, and have a speed of 30 knots. They eventually reached a standard displacement of 41,700 tons, making them comparable to the *Hood* in both size and armament.

The Admiralty rushed to complete the design of their new 35,000-ton entry into the battleship race. Several alternative armament systems were under consideration, including guns ranging in calibre from 14in to 16in and a variety of mounting configurations. The 16in guns aboard *Nelson* and *Rodney* had initially suffered from excessive wear of the gun tubes, which was only partially overcome by reducing the muzzle velocity. In addition to other problems associated with the turret system, the stresses and blast effect created by firing broadsides with all nine 16in guns located in the same area also caused difficulties, so that calibre was rejected. The 15in

2–2 The forward turrets of HMS *King George V*, photographed in October 1940. This class were the only British warships with quadruple turrets. (Imperial War Museum: A1488)

The New Generation

gun was the current standard of the Royal Navy, and the selection of that calibre for the new ships would minimise logistics problems with respect to ammunition and spares. As well as the traditional arrangement of eight 15in guns mounted in four twin turrets, mounting nine 15in guns in three triple turrets was another possibility that was considered.

However, the British believed that a calibre of 14in was the heaviest that could be supported by a properly armoured ship of 35,000 tons displacement, and during the London Naval Treaty negotiations, they proposed this calibre as the maximum main armament for new naval construction. The Japanese seemed willing to support this proposal, but the United States insisted on retaining the original 16in calibre limitation imposed by the Washington Naval Treaty. Although the United States position won out in the final London Naval Treaty, the Admiralty decided to go ahead with a new 14in gun system as the main armament for their new generation of battleships.

The 14in shells to be used with these new guns were to be of an improved type that would have better ballistic performance and greater armour-piercing capability than previous shells of this calibre. These new projectiles, however, would each weigh only 1600lbs compared with 1920lbs for the standard 15in shell. Although a 14in shell did not have the same damage potential of the heavier calibre, the lighter guns would allow a larger number of guns to be employed. A salvo of ten to twelve 14in guns would have a correspondingly greater probability of a hit than a salvo of only eight 15in guns.

At first, the Admiralty specified twelve 14in guns to be mounted in three quadruple turrets, two forward and one aft, but with weight becoming an issue in the final design of these ships, two guns were sacrificed in the interests of improved armour protection and speed and it was therefore decided that the armament layout would be a quadruple turret forward with a twin turret superfiring above it, and a quadruple turret aft. Ten 14in guns would still give these ships a broadside weight of about 7.9 tons, which was somewhat greater that the broadside weight of eight 15in guns mounted on other British battleships (7.7 tons) and significantly greater than the broadside weight of the *Bismarck* (7.1 tons).

The Bismarck Chase

Although problems were initially experienced with the quadruple mounting for the 14in gun, these were eventually corrected. Another concern was the weapon's relatively slow rate of fire – only 1.5 rounds per minute (one round every 40 seconds). In comparison, the standard British 15in gun system could fire at a rate of 2 rounds per minute (one round every 30 seconds). Of even greater significance was the more rapid rate of fire of 2.5 rounds per minute (one round every 25 seconds) for the German battleships *Bismarck* and *Tirpitz*.

The British waited for the expiry of the London Naval Treaty on 31 December 1936 which would end the moratorium on capital ship construction. On New Year's Day in 1937, they laid down their first two new generation 35,000-ton battleships, the *King George V* and *Prince of Wales*. The *King George V* was built by Vickers-Armstrong at Walker on the Tyne, and the *Prince of Wales* was built at the Birkenhead yard of Cammell Laird across the Mersey from Liverpool. The *King George V* was launched in February 1939 and completed in the autumn of 1940. During the first part of 1941, she was assigned to the Home Fleet stationed at Scapa Flow and was involved in escorting convoys from North America to the British Isles.

The *King George V* and *Prince of Wales* were followed in the same year by three more ships of the same class. The *Duke of York* was laid down in May 1937 in the John Brown Shipyard at Clydebank near Glasgow, Scotland. John Brown had earlier built the battlecruiser *Hood* as well as the liners *Queen Mary* and *Queen Elizabeth*. The *Anson* was laid down in July 1937 in the Swan Hunter Shipyard at Wallsend on the River Tyne near Newcastle, and the *Howe* was laid down in June 1937 in the Fairfield Shipyard at Govan on the Clyde.

The *King George V* class had an overall length of 745ft, a beam of 104ft, a standard draught of 29ft, and a speed of 28 knots. While the British made a sincere effort to hold down the displacement of these ships to the prescribed limit of 35,000 tons, their actual standard displacement slightly exceeded that figure at first and was further increased as wartime modifications were incorporated. In contrast, the *Bismarck* and *Tirpitz* already had an initial standard displacement of 41,700 tons on completion.

The New Generation

2–3 HMS *King George V* as she appeared in mid-1941. (Imperial War Museum: A6156)

The United States did not wait long after the end of the moratorium on capital ship construction before its own construction was renewed. In 1937, the 35,000-ton battleship *North Carolina* was laid down, followed by her sister ship, the *Washington*, in 1938. These ships had an overall length of 730ft, beam of 108ft, and draught of 27ft. They carried nine 16in guns in triple turrets, two forward and one aft, and twenty 5in dual-purpose guns in twin mounts along both sides of the ship. They also carried three aircraft

2–4 HMS *Prince of Wales* at Scapa Flow in 1941. (Imperial War Museum: A3869)

and had a speed of 28 knots. These ships were soon followed by four ships of the *South Dakota* class, which also displaced 35,000 tons and carried nine 16in guns. The *South Dakota* class battleships were somewhat shorter than the *North Carolina* class (680ft), which gave them a more compact appearance, but they were otherwise comparable to their earlier cousins.

Although they initially seemed to favour the British proposal to limit the calibre of main armament to 14in, the Japanese had been secretly planning for the construction of several huge battleships

The New Generation

mounting 18.1in guns, the largest-calibre guns ever to be installed on a capital ship. The British had used 18in guns in the First World War, but only on a few monitors and the 'light battlecruiser' *Furious*, which mounted a single gun of that calibre aft. The Japanese began work on two of these mammoth ships soon after the expiration of the London Naval Treaty. The *Yamato* was laid down in November 1937, and her sister-ship, the *Musashi*, followed in March 1938. These ships would displace over 60,000 tons and have a speed of 27 knots. They would have an overall length of 840ft, a beam of over 120ft, and a draught of 35ft. As completed, they would carry nine 18.1in guns in three triple turrets, two forward and one aft, a secondary battery of twelve 6.1in guns in four triple turrets and a variety of AA guns.

The *Prince of Wales* was launched on 3 May 1939, and was theoretically completed on 31 March 1941. She had already been formally commissioned into the Royal Navy on 19 January 1941, but she was still not considered to be fully operational. In the early part

2–5 Captain John C Leach, captain of the *Prince of Wales*, who later went down with his ship on 10 December 1941 when she was sunk by Japanese aircraft. (Imperial War Museum: H12775)

of May 1941, sea trials were conducted, and she then sailed to Scapa Flow for gunnery practice. She was still experiencing problems with her new 14in gun mounts, and three contractor technicians from Vickers-Armstrong remained on board during that period to assist in making them fully operational.

By mid-May, the threat of the *Bismarck* becoming operational and breaking out into the North Atlantic became a distinct possibility. On 21 May 1941, after receipt of the news that the *Bismarck* was already in Norwegian waters and poised to strike out into the North Atlantic, the *Prince of Wales* was abruptly declared operational and ordered to prepare for immediate departure.

Late in the evening of 21 May, the *Prince of Wales*, together with the battlecruiser *Hood* and six destroyers, set sail from Scapa Flow to take up a position south of Iceland. There they could intercept the *Bismarck* should she attempt to break out into the North Atlantic in either direction around that island. The *Prince of Wales* sailed with a crew of 1640 officers and men under the command of Captain John C Leach. In addition, she still had the Vickers-Armstrong technicians aboard, continuing their efforts to resolving the problems associated with the main armament.

CHAPTER 3

The Rebirth of German Seapower – Bismarck

At the end of the First World War, Germany surrendered nearly all of her warships to the Allied forces under the terms of the Armistice. Her High Seas Fleet of battleships and battlecruisers was interned at Scapa Flow awaiting disposition. Since a peace treaty had not yet been signed, Germany was technically still at war. In view of the possibility that their ships could be seized by the British and used against the Fatherland, on 21 June 1919 the German crews scuttled their ships. The British were able to save only one, the battleship *Baden*, by beaching her before she could sink.

Under the Treaty of Versailles, Germany was allowed to keep only eight obsolete pre-Dreadnought battleships, eight light cruisers, twelve destroyers, and twenty torpedo boats, but the restriction on manpower to only 15,000 meant that not all of these ships could be operated at any one time. Of the capital ships, only the battleships *Schlesien* and *Schleswig-Holstein* remained in service until the Second World War. These 13,200-ton ships were laid down in 1905 and completed in 1908. They carried four 11in guns in two twin turrets, one forward and one aft, and had a speed of 18 knots. Although they were suitable only for coastal defence and training purposes, the *Schleswig-Holstein* did have the distinction of firing the opening shots of the Second World War when she bombarded the Polish fortress of Westerplatte guarding the harbour of Danzig (modern Gdansk) in the early morning of 1 September 1939.

Germany was allowed to build replacement ships, but they could not exceed 10,000 tons in displacement and could not have guns exceeding 11in in calibre. This posed quite a challenge to German naval architects. How could they design a capital ship with those

The Bismarck Chase

3-1 The panzerschiff ('pocket battleship') *Admiral Scheer* passing through the Kiel Canal before the outbreak of war. Note the layout of her armament and the tower bridge. (Imperial War Museum: HU1035)

limitations, squeezing the features of a battleship into the hull of a cruiser? They considered all of the factors involved, came up with several alternative designs, and finally decided on a unique solution. No such ship had ever before been conceived, so the Germans merely called it *'Panzerschiff'* (armoured ship). The world would soon come to know that type of ship by the term 'pocket battleship'.

Although the displacement of the pocket battleships was officially 10,000 tons, and considerable weight savings were made by having fully-welded hulls, all the ships of this class significantly exceeded the Treaty limits, which was kept secret by the Germans. Each ship was be propelled by eight diesel engines and two screws that would drive the ships at a speed of 26 knots. They would have an overall length of 610ft, beam of 69ft, and draught of 19ft. Their armament comprised six 11in guns in two triple turrets, one forward and one aft, and a secondary armament of eight 5.9in guns in single mounts, four on either side of the ship along the main deck. The last two ships would also carry eight 21in torpedo tubes in two quadruple mounts on the afterdeck, as well as two aircraft. Although Germany had some experience with triple turrets on her latest light cruisers, the development of such mountings for the 11in gun was a significant technical achievement.

The first pocket battleship, the *Deutschland*, was laid down in February 1929, launched in May 1931, and completed in April 1933. She was followed by two ships of an improved design, the *Admiral Scheer*, completed in 1934, and finally the *Admiral Graf Spee*, completed in 1936. The *Deutschland* had a curved bridge structure that made her look more like a cruise liner than a warship. She also had a relatively thin cylindrical structure behind the bridge to support the forward rangefinder. In contrast the *Admiral Scheer* and *Admiral Graf Spee* had massive square-shaped towers. They also had their forward fire control directors placed on a second deck forward of the bridge tower instead of behind the bridge as aboard the *Deutschland*.

The tower bridges of the *Admiral Scheer* and the *Admiral Graf Spee* also accommodated searchlights, communications equipment, and a variety of other combat support functions previously relegated to spaces below deck. This tower design was carried forward into all later major German warships built before and during the Second World War. A similar structure was also incorporated into all of the new battleships and battlecruisers built by the United States, in lieu of the wire-cage and tripod mast designs used on earlier battleships for their forward and aft fire control stations. Several of the American battleships refitted during the Second World War were also modified along these lines.

The characteristics of these pocket battleships seemingly made them ideal hit-and-run commerce raiders, being able to outrun any battleship with superior armament and outshoot any cruiser with superior speed. These characteristics would be put to the test early in the Second World War when two of the pocket battleships were immediately sent out on raiding missions. The *Deutschland*, operating in the North Atlantic, had only limited success in sinking two merchant ships and capturing a third before she had to return to port due to mechanical problems. The *Admiral Graf Spee* sank nine merchant ships before she was finally intercepted by a force of three

British cruisers in the South Atlantic off the coast of Uruguay in December 1939. Although she severely damaged the heavy cruiser, HMS *Exeter* during the initial stage of the battle, the *Admiral Graf Spee* was herself damaged by the combined firepower of the light cruisers, HMS *Ajax* and HMNZS *Achilles*. Driven to seek shelter in the port of Montevideo, the *Admiral Graf Spee* was scuttled in that harbour on 17 December 1939 rather than face the force of British warships her captain feared were mustered in the mouth of the River Plate.

The Allies tried to argue Germany out of building pocket battleships, but she refused on the grounds that she had been excluded from the London Naval Treaty of 1930. France responded by building two new fast battleships, the *Dunkerque* and *Strasbourg*, which would be superior to any *Panzerschiff* in both armament and speed (see Chapter 2).

Adolf Hitler was appointed Chancellor of Germany by President Hindenburg in 1933. When Hindenburg died a year later, Hitler took over complete control of the government as the *Führer* (leader) of Germany. He soon renounced the Treaty of Versailles and began a rearmament programme to re-establish Germany as a major power. The German Naval High Command already had designs on the drawing boards for ships exceeding the Versailles limitations, and on the direction of the Nazi regime, it took immediate action to initiate a major naval shipbuilding programme. The Germans finalised plans for two new 26,000-ton battleships that would mount nine 11in guns in three triple turrets, two forward and one aft, and ordered the materials for their construction.

The battleship *Gneisenau* was laid down in May 1935, launched in December 1936, and commissioned in May 1938. She was followed by a sister ship, the *Scharnhorst*, which was also laid down in May 1935, but was launched in October 1936 and not commissioned until January 1939. At time of their completion, both ships had a standard displacement of 31,000 tons. They had an overall length of 742ft, beam of 98ft, and draught of 28ft. Their steam turbines geared to three shafts could drive the ships at a speed of 30 knots. In addition to their main armament, they also carried twelve 5.9in guns in four twin mounts and four single mounts (six guns on each side), and numerous AA guns.

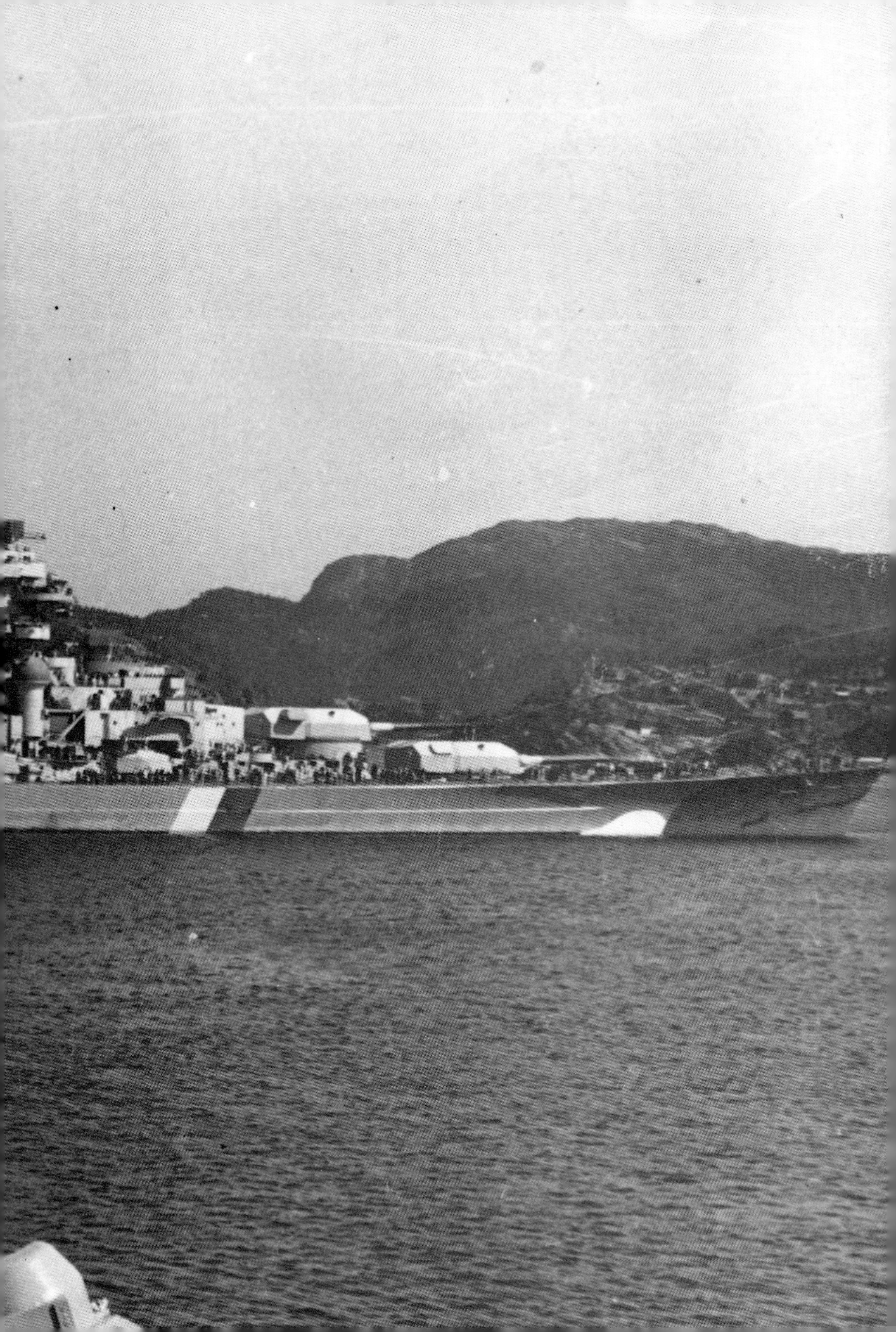

The Bismarck Chase

4-4 Admiral Günther Lütjens, flag officer commanding *Bismarck* and *Prinz Eugen* during Operation 'Rhine Exercise'. (Imperial War Museum: A14897)

he was given the 'green light' to proceed. Two days later, he briefed the officers of the *Bismarck* and *Prinz Eugen* on his intentions.

In the afternoon of Sunday 18 May, the *Bismarck* and *Prinz Eugen* steamed out of the harbour of Gotenhafen to the strains of a band playing patriotic tunes. The ships went only a short distance before dropping anchor outside the harbour where they were refuelled and took on additional provisions from awaiting barges. They finally got underway in the early morning hours of 19 May. The ships first circled around the Hel Peninsula, a thin finger of land jutting down from the Baltic coast, and then headed westward.

The *Bismarck* had a normal crew of about 2060 officers and men. In addition, she carried a number of Luftwaffe pilots and mechanics for the aircraft on board. But by the time she sailed, her complement was increased to over 2200 men, making it difficult to find accommodation for so many. The additional personnel included the staff for the fleet commander, prize crews for captured merchant ships, midshipmen assigned for training, and war correspondents intent on capturing the battleship's glorious exploits.

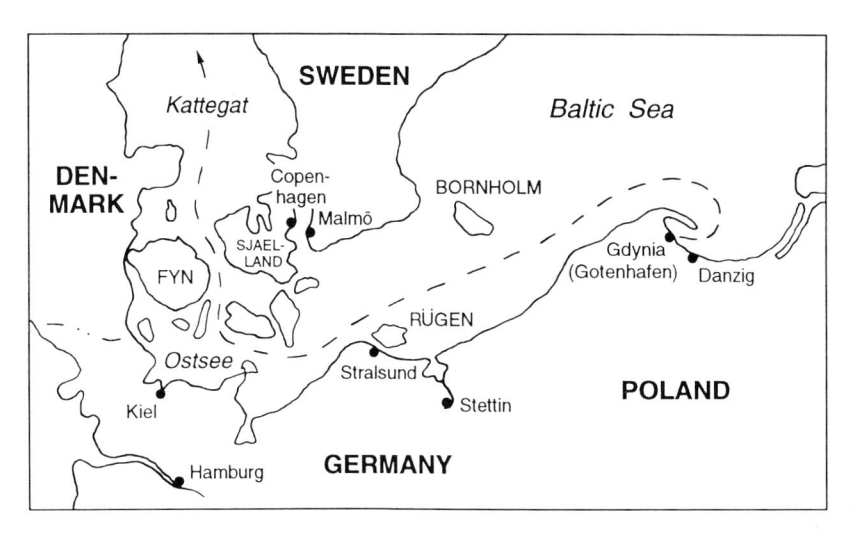

4–5 Route of *Bismarck* and *Prinz Eugen* from Gdynia (Gotenhafen) to the Kattegat.

By nightfall the task force, escorted by two destroyers, reached the western end of the Baltic Sea and turned north to pass through the Great Belt between the Danish islands of Fyn and Sjaelland, on which Copenhagen is located. On the following morning of 20 May, the *Bismarck* and the *Prinz Eugen* had reached the Kattegat, and they were soon off the coast of neutral Sweden amid a fleet of Danish and Swedish fishing boats. Shortly after noon, the ships came across the Swedish cruiser *Gotland* on patrol between the Kattegat and Skaggerak, which immediately radioed a sighting report to Naval Headquarters in Stockholm. After clearing the northern tip of Denmark, the German ships headed west through the Skaggerak toward the North Sea and the Atlantic.

During the night of 20 May, the *Bismarck* and *Prinz Eugen* rounded the southern coast of Norway near Kristiansand and headed north-west toward Stavanger, which they reached at about dawn on the morning of 21 May. Just before noon, they entered the shipping channel of Korsfjord and slowly steamed north through the fjord toward Bergen, Norway. The *Bismarck* turned into Grimstadfjord and anchored in a cove at the eastern end of that fjord south-west of Bergen. The *Prinz Eugen* and the accompanying destroyers continued northward to the southern end of Hjeltefjord,

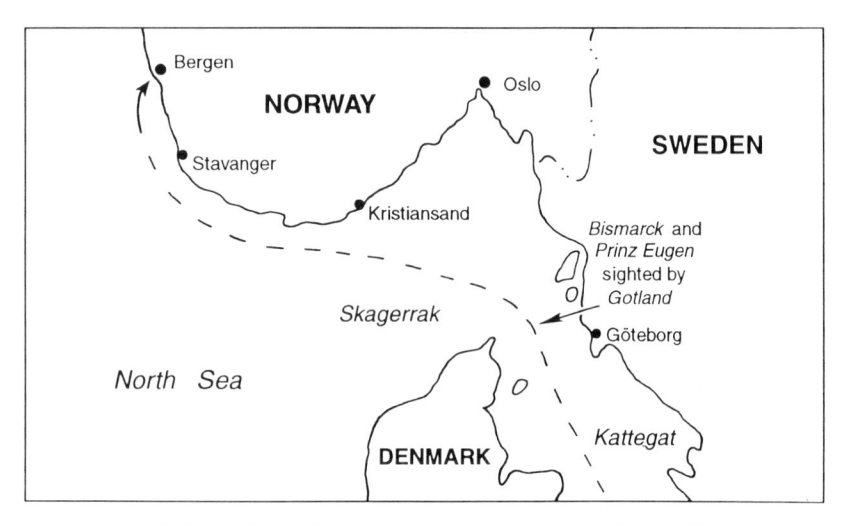

4–6 Route of *Bismarck* and *Prinz Eugen* from the Kattegat to Bergen, Norway.

and there they dropped anchor in a cove between the headlands of Kalvanes and Vickenes, sometimes referred to as Kalvanes Bay.

While at their anchorages, both ships were repainted overall in an dark grey colour more fitting for operations in the North Atlantic. Both took on additional supplies, and the *Prinz Eugen* topped off her fuel tanks, but the *Bismarck* did not. Lütjens was briefed on the latest intelligence that the Germans had regarding the disposition of British warships at Scapa Flow and along the possible routes that his ships could take in breaking out into the North Atlantic. As far as was known, all units of the Home Fleet were still at their base at Scapa Flow, and there appeared to be no serious threat to the breakout along the more northerly routes that he could take.

Lütjens theoretically had a choice of four different ways into the North Atlantic. The nearest route was the passage between the Orkney Islands off the northern coast of Scotland and the Shetland Islands, a little further north-east of the Orkney Islands. This route was rejected out of hand due to its proximity to the British naval base at Scapa Flow and RAF bases in northern Scotland. The route between the Shetland Island and the Danish Faeroe Islands was not much better for essentially the same reasons. The only truly viable alternatives were either the passage between the Faeroe Islands and

The British Response

Denmark Strait at the north-west corner of the island. Two additional bases, Seydisfjord (Seydisfjördur) and Reydarfjord (Reydarfjördur), are located on the east coast. Seydisfjord, the largest town on that coast, is at the head of the fjord bearing the same name. It was linked to the Shetland Islands by a submarine cable laid in 1906 and now also by a ferry. Reydarfjord, a small village at the head of that fjord, is located about 20 miles south of Seydisfjord. These fjords were large enough to serve as anchorages for British warships being serviced at those bases.

Recognising that the Denmark Strait would be one of the primary passages used by German raiders and supply ships, the British had laid several minefields off the north-western coast of Iceland. This reduced the navigable width of the channel to just a few miles which could be covered more easily by their patrols. German intelligence was aware of the existence of these minefields, but they also knew that the minefields did not extend all the way to the fringe of the pack ice off the coast of Greenland. This left a narrow channel that was relatively safe for their ships to transit.

As an earlier precaution, the Admiralty had already alerted the heavy cruisers, *Norfolk* and *Suffolk*, on patrol in the Denmark Strait, of the possibility of a breakout by the *Bismarck* through that passage. These ships were under Rear-Admiral William F Wake-Walker, flag officer commanding the First Cruiser Squadron, who flew his flag in the *Norfolk*. The *Suffolk* had been on station at the northern end of the Denmark Strait for several days, and she was running low on fuel. The *Norfolk*, then refuelling at Hvalfjord, was ordered to relieve the *Suffolk* so that she too could be refuelled and made ready for extended operations.

The *Norfolk* and *Suffolk* were 'County' class cruisers, and were distinguishable by their three funnels. The *Norfolk* was one of two ships of the *Norfolk*-class, and the *Suffolk* was one of seven *Kent*-class cruisers. They were all built in the late 1920s and displaced about 10,000 tons. They had an overall length of 630ft, beam of 68ft, and draught of 16ft, and they could travel at a speed of 31 knots. They carried eight 8in guns in four twin turrets, two forward and two aft, eight 21in torpedo tubes in two quadruple mounts, and an anti-aircraft battery of four 4in guns. While not as large or as modern as the *Prinz Eugen*, they were otherwise generally comparable to the German heavy cruiser in armament, speed, and armour protection.

In addition to alerting these two ships in the Denmark Strait, the Admiralty took further precautionary action based on the sighting report from Stockholm. Admiral Sir John C Tovey, Commander-in-Chief of the British Home Fleet stationed at Scapa Flow, was authorised to use all of the assets at his disposal to prevent the breakout of the *Bismarck* into the North Atlantic. This included the battleships *King George V* and *Prince of Wales*, the battlecruisers *Hood* and *Repulse*, the aircraft carrier *Victorious*, several cruisers, and a host of destroyers. While not actually part of the Home Fleet, the *Repulse* and *Victorious* were in the area and were therefore placed under Admiral Tovey's control.

The *Repulse* was one of the two battlecruisers besides the *Hood* that the Royal Navy retained after the First World War. She was laid down at the John Brown Shipyard at Clydebank near Glasgow, Scotland in January 1915, launched 12 months later, and completed in August 1916. In 1933 she had entered Portsmouth Dockyard for an extensive rebuild, including increased deck armour and an improved anti-aircraft battery. In 1941 her main armament was unchanged at six 15in guns in three triple turrets, two forward and one aft, but time and increased displacement had reduced her original speed of 30 knots to 28 knots.

The *Victorious* was one of six new fleet aircraft carriers laid down between 1937 and 1939. She was built by Vickers-Armstrong (Tyne) near Newcastle and just completed mid-May 1941. She displaced 23,000 tons and had a speed of 30 knots. She had an overall length of nearly 750ft, beam of 96ft, and draught of 24ft. She could carry only 36 aircraft, since hangar space had been sacrificed to give her class better protection against air attacks. She had a battery of sixteen 4.5in guns in twin mounts as well as numerous smaller-calibre AA guns.

It now became the task of Admiral Tovey to deploy the resources placed under his command to stop the *Bismarck*. Tackling the German battleship on a one-for-one basis seemed to be out of the question. The *Bismarck* was the ultimate product of German naval

The British Response

5–2 Admiral Sir John C Tovey, Commander-in-Chief Home Fleet, aboard his flagship HMS *King George V*. (Imperial War Museum: A14840)

technology and recent training had undoubtedly honed her crew up to the razor's edge of perfection. Tovey's flagship, the *King George V*, was the only ship in the Royal Navy that had anything like an even chance to stand up to the her alone, by virtue of her modern construction and crew experience. Tovey realised, however, that the Germans had probably crammed every advantage into the *Bismarck* regardless of international restrictions while the British made a sincere effort to keep their new capital ships within treaty limits.

The *Prince of Wales*, sister ship of the *King George V*, had just been commissioned two months earlier. Technical problems with her main armament had not as yet been corrected and she was still undergoing repairs by contractor personnel. While some members of her crew had been drawn from other ships to form an experienced cadre, others came directly from basic seamen's training programmes or were recent graduates of naval technical schools. They were undoubtedly well qualified to perform their assigned tasks, but there had been little opportunity for the crew members to train together and form a coherent fighting force. That ruled out her as being able to take on the *Bismarck* alone.

The *Hood* had the next best chance of challenging the *Bismarck* by herself. She was comparable to her opponent in size, armament, and speed, and her crew was well trained and had actual combat experience against the French at Oran just a year earlier. But the battlecruiser was of First World War vintage, and despite numerous refits during the intervening years, was still not up to the standards of a modern warship. Her greatest deficiency was, of course, the lack of adequate armour protection, especially on her horizontal surfaces. This made the *Hood* especially vulnerable to plunging fire at longer ranges.

The *Repulse* was certainly no match for the *Bismarck*. As a ship of the same vintage as the *Hood*, she had the same technical limitations as her larger cousin, although she had an equally well-trained crew which had seen action in the Norwegian campaign of 1940. She was also handicapped by her limited main armament. With only six 15in guns compared to eight for the *Bismarck*, she had only 75 per cent of the firepower of her enemy. The *Victorious* could be of help under circumstances that permitted air operations, but otherwise she had no firepower to contribute to a surface action.

Then there was the matter of *Bismarck*'s consort, most likely a heavy cruiser of the *Admiral Hipper*-class and probably the *Prinz Eugen*, the latest ship of that class. While her 8in guns would not be capable of inflicting mortal damage to a capital ship, they could included the battleship *King George V*, aircraft carrier *Victorious*, light cruisers *Aurora, Galatea, Hermione, Kenya,* and *Neptune*, and six destroyers. With his flag in the *King George V*, Tovey left port some time before midnight on 22 May. The *Repulse*, about to embark on convoy duty, was recalled from the Firth of Clyde near Glasgow and ordered to join Admiral Tovey's force at sea north-west of Scotland. There the task force would lie in wait behind the light cruiser screen, ready to pounce on the *Bismarck* should she attempt the Iceland-Faeroes passage, or be prepared to turn westward and support the *Hood-Prince of Wales* task force should the Germans come through the Denmark Strait.

Everything that could be done in preparation for the expected breakout attempt by the *Bismarck* and her consort had been done. In addition to the deployment of the Home Fleet, Force H at Gibraltar was alerted for possible later support should the German squadron succeed in breaking out. Convoys in the North Atlantic and their naval escorts were also alerted to the possible new danger that they might face under those circumstances. Now it became a waiting game until the *Bismarck* could be located and the entire weight of the Royal Navy concentrated toward her destruction. The patrolling cruisers were on full alert, ready to report any sign of the German ships, and the two battlegroups were ready to respond to any sighting of them. Coverage of the two remaining passages, *ie*, Orkneys-Shetlands and Shetlands-Faeroes, was left to the RAF in the unlikely event that the *Bismarck* and *Prinz Eugen* would attempt a breakout so close to the British Isles.

CHAPTER 6

Initial Contact

The *Bismarck* and *Prinz Eugen* continued to sail westward toward the northern entrance of the Denmark Strait, totally unaware that they had been discovered at Bergen, or that the Home Fleet had been deployed to intercept them. German reconnaissance flights over Scapa Flow had failed to reveal the departure of major units of the Home Fleet. Not even the bombing raid on the vacant fjord after their departure from Norwegian waters was interpreted as an indication that the *Bismarck* had possibly been discovered. Admiral Lütjens was left to proceed on his own to accomplish a dangerous mission without the essential intelligence about the enemy that should have been provided to him by the High Command.

By the late afternoon of 23 May, the *Bismarck* and *Prinz Eugen* were approaching the pack ice off the coast of Greenland. From there, they turned on a south-westerly course and steamed into the fog-shrouded northern entrance of the Denmark Strait with the *Bismarck* in the lead. The Germans were aware from their intelligence reports that minefields had been laid off the north-west coast of Iceland in the Denmark Strait, but they did not know exactly where those minefields were. With the channel already narrowed by the pack ice, it became a very tricky operation to negotiate the passage.

The German squadron proceeded cautiously down the dangerous channel during the rest of the afternoon. In the early evening, at about 1920, they made contact with the British heavy cruiser *Suffolk*, which had been patrolling in that area. As soon as her lookouts spotted the German ships, the *Suffolk* turned toward the coast of Iceland for the protection of the fog. Knowing the exact location of the minefield in that area, the cruiser was able to take refuge in one of the safe passages left open in it. After transmitting a

Initial Contact

0200, an hour or so before the Germans could reach that point. With sunset occurring about that same time at 65° North Latitude, the German ships would be silhouetted in the afterglow for half an hour before full darkness set in.

The British had a two-to-one superiority over the German squadron in ships and nearly a two-to-one advantage in firepower. Table 6–1 shows the relative firepower of the two opposing forces in terms of the weight of shells that could be hurled against the enemy force each minute. While this looked impressive on paper, the British superiority was actually diminished by the age and relative combat effectiveness of their ships. While nearly equal in firepower to the *Bismarck*, the *Hood* was a much older ship and was more vulnerable than her German counterpart. In terms of combat effectiveness, they were about equal. The *Hood* had a highly experienced crew that had already seen combat while the crew of the *Bismarck* had been honed to the highest level of proficiency by recent training.

The *Prince of Wales'* firepower added to the British side of the equation, but she was a new ship and not yet in a state of full combat readiness and was still having difficulty with the functioning of her main armament. The two British cruisers following the German squadron each approximated the *Prinz Eugen* in firepower,

Table 6–1: Comparison of Main Armament Firepower between British and German Forces

Ships	Calibre of Guns (in)	Rate of Fire (rounds per minute)	Number of guns	Weight of shell (lbs)	Firepower (tons per minute)
British					
Hood	15	2.0	8	1920	15.4
Pr Wales	14	1.5	10	1590	11.9
Norfolk	8	6.0	8	256	6.1
Suffolk	8	6.0	8	256	6.1
TOTAL					39.5
German					
Bismarck	15	2.5	8	1760	17.6
Prinz Eugen	8	4.0	8	270	4.3
TOTAL					21.9

but they were also old ships and not quite equal to their somewhat larger German counterpart. Although nominally 10,000 tons, the *Prinz Eugen* actually displaced over 14,000 tons and was 50ft longer and 4ft wider than the *Suffolk* and *Norfolk*.

Holland had ideal conditions whereby he could steam across the path of the oncoming German squadron, crossing the 'T' in the traditional naval manoeuvre that would have give him a tremendous advantage over the enemy. With this, he could place the *Hood* and *Prince of Wales* in a position where they could block the German squadron and bring their full broadsides to bear on the *Bismarck*, which would be able to use only her forward turrets. That would give the British force a nearly four-to-one advantage in firepower and almost assure the destruction of the *Bismarck* as the range continued to close.

If the *Bismarck* turned broadside-on, the British would still have a two-to-one superiority in firepower and be able to split her fire. If she turned tail and ran back into the Denmark Strait, the British would have accomplished their primary objective of keeping the Germans from breaking out into the North Atlantic, and she could be taken care of later. In the meanwhile, the *Suffolk* and *Norfolk*, coming up from the rear, would be in a position to jointly take on the *Prinz Eugen* at two-to-one odds.

During the remainder of the evening, both forces continued on their convergent courses with the *Suffolk* periodically reporting the position of the German squadron to the Admiralty as well as to Holland on the *Hood* and Tovey on *King George V*. The Germans made several attempts during the night to shake their pursuers, but to no avail. At about 2200, the *Bismarck* doubled back on her course hoping to catch the British cruisers by surprise, but they were nowhere in sight. The *Suffolk* had detected the manoeuvre on her radar, and both cruisers disappeared in the fog as the German ships approached. When the *Bismarck* returned to her original course, the two cruisers resumed their shadowing duties astern of the German squadron

At about midnight, the German ships came upon a snowstorm that interfered with the *Suffolk*'s radar reception and she lost contact with them. When contact had not been regained after an hour,

Initial Contact

Admiral Holland decided to turn in a more northerly direction in an attempt to intercept the *Bismarck* in case his quarry turned south while hidden from radar contact. It was a difficult decision for him to make, but he could not afford to have the German squadron come down astern of him and break out into the North Atlantic. When contact had still not made by 0200, Admiral Holland turned to a south-westerly course, still hoping to cut the *Bismarck* off before the onset of total darkness.

At about 0300, *Suffolk* finally regained radar contact with the German squadron. The *Bismarck* and *Prinz Eugen* had actually maintained their original course all along, so the manoeuvre by Admiral Holland turned out to have been unnecessary. Apparently Lütjens had wanted to keep a wide berth between himself and any additional British warships that might approach him from the east. He therefore kept on a course of about 220° parallel to the coast of Greenland. This gave him limited space to manoeuvre to the west in the event of an encounter with heavy units of the Royal Navy due to the presence of pack ice off the coast, but it would take longer for any British ships to reach him.

Holland must have been dismayed by this unfortunate turn of events and its consequences. His precautionary move of turning to the north when contact with the Germans was lost cost him precious time, and he had missed his opportunity of being able to cut in front of the *Bismarck*. He still had a slight lead over the German squadron, so there was no question of not being able to intercept them, but he was no longer far enough ahead of them to execute the 'crossing the T' manoeuvre that he had hoped for. This reduced his advantage considerably and would have a critical impact on the forthcoming battle.

Not wanting to engage in darkness, Holland ordered his task force to steer a course that would allow for the interception of the *Bismarck* as soon as it became light. The *Hood* and *Prince of Wales* kept up a good pace to ensure they would still be able to engage the German squadron at dawn. Their escorting destroyers, however, had difficulty maintaining that speed in the heavy seas of the North Atlantic, so they were allowed to drop back and follow the battle group as best they could. This was unfortunate since that would

6–2 HMS *Hood* photographed from HMS *Prince of Wales* on 23 May 1941, racing to intercept the *Bismarck*. (Imperial War Museum: HU70156)

leave the destroyers more than an hour's steaming time from the rest of the task force by dawn.

The crews of the *Hood* and *Prince of Wales* understood what they would be up against at daybreak. They knew that the *Bismarck* would be at its peak fighting trim, and they recognised their own limitations. Theoretically, they would have the enemy outnumbered and outgunned, and that gave them some comfort. On the other hand, the *Hood* was an old ship that could be vulnerable to the devastating fire expected from the *Bismarck*. The crew of the *Prince of Wales* recognised that their ship was not yet at full efficiency, both mechanically and from the viewpoint of their own combat proficiency. While they were individually highly qualified, they had not had sufficient time to train together as an team or with other ships as an integrated task force.

The crews of the *Bismarck* and *Prinz Eugen*, on the other hand, were blissfully ignorant of the tremendous naval power that was being amassed against them. They were concerned about the cruisers that were dogging them, but they had the utmost confidence in their ability to handle anything that they might encounter. In the *Bismarck*, they had the most powerful battleship in the world, and the *Prinz Eugen* had no peer as a heavy cruiser. Their morale was high, and they were prepared to give their all for the Fatherland. Their fleet commander, however, certainly must have had some apprehension as to what lay ahead.

Lütjens knew of course that his position had been radioed to the Admiralty and that all the available resources of the Royal Navy were being mustered against him. He did not know, however, how much of a head start he had. He was not aware that his passage through the Kattegat had been leaked to the British, although that was a possibility that he had to consider, especially after encountering so many fishing vessels in that area. Furthermore, he did not know that his ships had been photographed at their anchorages near Bergen by the RAF, nor that his departure had been detected on the following day. He did not know of the whereabouts of the Home Fleet and therefore had absolutely no idea what would be in store for him in the morning.

CHAPTER 7

Enemy in Sight

Once contact had been re-established with the German squadron and its position became known, Holland could not afford to relax the state of readiness of his ships. The British had to be prepared in case the *Bismarck* and *Prinz Eugen* took an unexpected turn south and closed the gap between the two forces more rapidly. It would only be a couple of hours before visual contact was expected with the enemy, so the remaining time was spent in checking out equipment and making other preparations for the forthcoming battle, such as fire-fighting and damage control. The crews of the *Hood* and *Prince of Wales* would have to eat and get what rest they could at their battle stations.

As dawn approached, the crews were put on full alert. With both forces steaming on convergent courses, it would be only a matter of time before visual contact was made with the German squadron. Lookouts trained their glasses to starboard along the horizon to catch the first glimpse of the oncoming German ships. Finally, at 0537, just as dawn was breaking, one of the lookouts spotted a tiny speck on the horizon almost directly off the starboard beam. Then a second speck appeared. The *Bismarck* and the *Prinz Eugen* had both been sighted at a distance of about 30,000 yards (17 miles). With action imminent, 'Battle Stations' was sounded, and the crew members of both ships, already at their assigned posts, stood to their guns.

Although the guns of the British ships could shoot that far, the range of 30,000 yards was considered to be too great for effective fire (see Appendix A). The probability of a hit with a full salvo from eight to ten guns was less than 25 per cent at that range. A reasonable chance for hits could be expected only at ranges of 25,000 yards or less, with the odds increasing rapidly as the range decreased.

Enemy in Sight

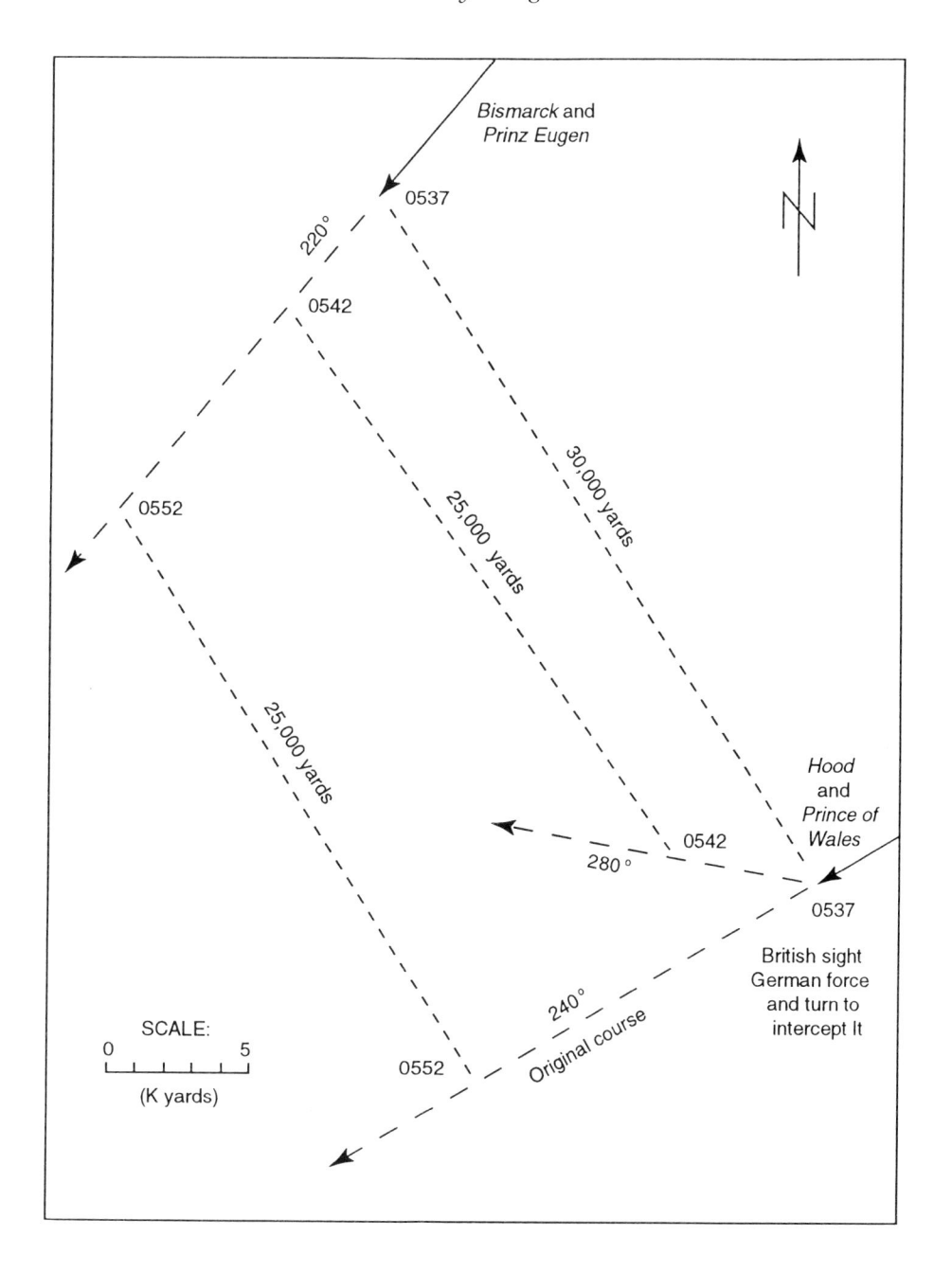

7–1 Position of British and German forces at time of sighting, and the first British turn.

As soon as the position, course, and speed of the German ships had been plotted, Holland quickly took stock of the situation. He still had a slight lead on the German squadron, sufficient to ensure that he could intercept the *Bismarck*, but his hope of being able to put his ships directly in front of the approaching German squadron would not be fulfilled. Instead, he would have to approach the enemy on a near-parallel course, but he still had a numerical advantage of two to one in ships and firepower. Had he been able to arrive on the scene only 30 minutes earlier, he would have been able to trap the German squadron and have a good chance of destroying it with minimum risk to his own force.

The British task force had been steaming on a course of 240° (west by south-west), while the German squadron was steering a course of 220° (almost directly south-west). The two forces were on almost parallel courses with only a 20° angle of convergence (*ie* the difference between the two courses). At this angle of convergence, the rate of closure was about 310 yards per minute. This meant that the British squadron would not be within effective range for another 15 minutes (or not until 0552) if both squadrons maintained their present course. Since Holland did have a slight lead over the German ships, he could take advantage this and bring the issue to a head sooner.

He ordered his ships to execute a 40° turn to starboard which put them on a new course of 280°. This increased the rate of closure to about 780 yards per minute and would put the *Bismarck* within effective range in only about 5 minutes (or by 0542). The German ships would be at a bearing of about 50–55°, which would give the *Hood* and *Prince of Wales* more than enough angle to bring their rear turrets to bear. The rear turrets of the British ships could be traversed forward up to 40–45° from the centreline of the ship measured away from the bow.

Aboard the *Bismarck*, Admiral Lütjens was reluctant to give his crews any respite during the early morning hours of 24 May. Not knowing what to expect, he kept the crews of both ships at their battle stations. He realised that the first few hours of daylight would be critical to the success of his mission and possibly even the survival of his squadron, and he wanted his men to be ready

Enemy in Sight

for any eventuality. He was still steaming parallel to the coast of Greenland at a bearing of about 220°, and with the pack ice only a short distance away, he had little manoeuvring room to starboard. Soon he would have sailed far enough to risk steering a more southerly course away from Greenland and have a better chance of avoiding any additional British forces that might be sent against him.

Shortly before dawn, the sensitive underwater sound detection apparatus aboard the *Prinz Eugen* began picking up the sound of ships some 20 miles to the south-east. This information was immediately signalled to the Admiral aboard *Bismarck*, who ordered lookouts on both German ships to scan the horizon in that direction. Lütjens had not received any new intelligence from the German Naval High Command regarding the disposition and movements of British naval units, so he could only speculate as to the nature of the ship or ships detected by the *Prinz Eugen*.

Finally, at about 0535, German lookouts spotted two wisps of smoke on the horizon in the direction indicated by the *Prinz Eugen*'s sound detection equipment. They were plotted to be about 20° forward of the port beam, which gave them a slight lead on the German squadron. The smoke obviously came from British warships brought on by the shadowing cruisers' sighting reports, but what type of ships were they? In all probability, they were two more cruisers called in to reinforce the *Suffolk* and *Norfolk* in their surveillance role. While this would not be a serious threat to the German squadron, it could make it more difficult for the Germans to shake off their pursuers.

The German Naval High Command had earlier advised Lütjens that the British Home Fleet was still at its anchorage at Scapa Flow, and he had no reason to believe that any units had left their base since then. It was therefore difficult for him to conceive that either or both of the two ships sighted were capital ships, but he could not ignore the possibility that at least one of them was. If that was the case, and the other was a cruiser, Lütjens was fully confident that his force could handle the situation, even though he would be outnumbered, with the addition of the two cruisers already pursuing him.

The Bismarck Chase

If, on the other hand, both ships were capital ships, that would pose greater problems. However, if they were two of the older battleships of the Royal Navy, such as the *Rodney* and *Royal Sovereign*, the German ships with their superior speed could easily turn to the west and then head south to cut around them. At first, they would be heading at an oblique angle to the Greenland coastline with its surrounding pack ice, but there would still be sufficient space to manoeuvre around the British force given their advantage in speed.

Another possibility was that the ships were two battlecruisers. Of the three battlecruisers in the Royal Navy, two of them, the *Renown* and the *Repulse*, were smaller ships carrying only six 15in guns. Together they could give the *Bismarck* some trouble by dividing her fire, but they were old and vulnerable ships and could easily be put out of action by a modern, more powerful battleship. The third battlecruiser was of course the mighty *Hood*, which was about the same size and carried the equivalent armament as the *Bismarck*. In company with one of the smaller battlecruisers, she could present a more formidable foe, but she was similarly old and vulnerable. All three of these battlecruisers could match or exceed the speed of the *Bismarck*.

The British had two new battleships, the *King George V* and *Prince of Wales*, each theoretically comparable to the *Bismarck* and capable of attaining about the same speed as the German ships. But the *Prince of Wales* was known to be still fitting out and her crew was not fully trained, so her availability was discounted. That left only the *King George V* as a serious threat to the *Bismarck*. She had been in service for 5 months, sufficient time to forge her crew into an effective fighting unit and to work out the mechanical problems common to any new ship.

The worst-case scenario from Lütjens' point of view was the *King George V* in concert with the *Hood*. The *King George V* was a modern ship with a well-trained crew and the *Hood* had been the mightiest warship in the world during the inter-war years, and she had already seen combat action in the Second World War. Her crew was battle-hardened and trained to the ultimate degree of proficiency in gunnery after decades of practice and recent combat

Enemy in Sight

experience. Together, they could pose a very real threat to the *Bismarck*, and the *Prinz Eugen* would certainly be hard-pressed to defend herself against both British heavy cruisers coming up from the rear.

Lütjens was under standing orders to avoid combat with British warships unless it was necessary to attack Allied merchant ships carrying war supplies to the British Isles. When it became apparent from the plot of the warships on the horizon that they were on a course to intercept him, Lütjens had no alternative but to turn away from them. He certainly had nothing to lose by taking such action. If those ships were in fact older British battleships, he could outrun them and eventually sail around them. If they were not, such a manoeuvre would at least give him more time to plan his strategy for dealing with this new threat.

Therefore, at about 0539, Lütjens ordered his squadron to execute a 45° turn to starboard on a new course of 265°, almost due west. He could not go in the opposite direction from the British force since that would lead him to a dead end at the edge of the pack ice off Greenland. The course he chose was a compromise which allowed his ships to take advantage of their superior speed in circling around the enemy force without completely giving up his

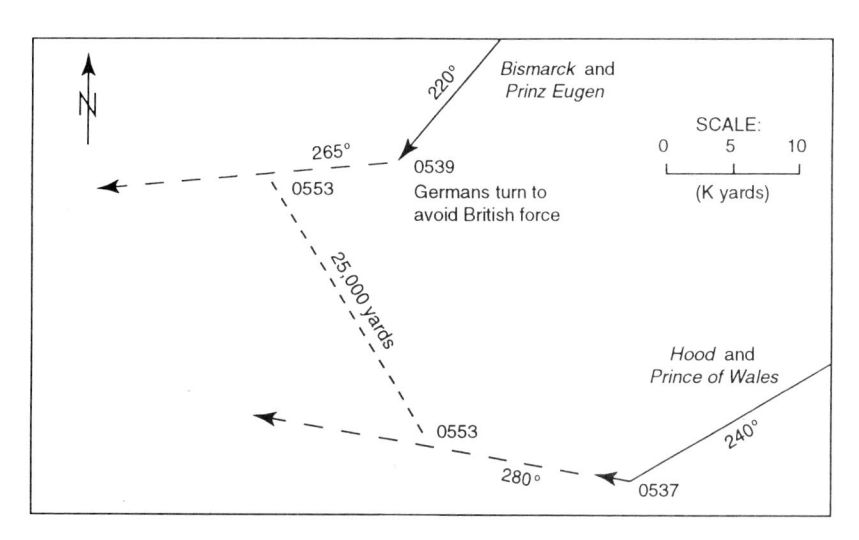

7–2 Germans turn to avoid British force and delay engagement until 0553.

manoeuvring room. The effect of this turn also reduced the rate of closure between the two forces to about 235 yards per minute and thereby delayed the inevitable clash between the opposing forces.

From now on it would be a waiting game to see what the British would do next. The gunners and spotters strained at their sights to pick up any details of the approaching ships that would aid in their identification, especially as to type and capabilities. The *Bismarck* had a 10m (33ft) stereoscopic rangefinder atop its tower superstructure, nearly 90ft above the waterline, and that provided the best possible view of the enemy. Lütjens continued to study the situation he faced and was anxiously awaiting word on the identity of the two new contacts so he could finalise his plan of action.

Within a couple of minutes, Holland realised that the German squadron had turned away from him, but there was little that he could do about it. Turning further toward the enemy would put his force in the rear of the German squadron, which was of course unacceptable. By maintaining his present course, he would still be in a position to intercept the *Bismarck*, but it would now take a little longer. The angle of convergence was down to only 15°, *ie* the difference between the courses of the British force (280°) and the German squadron (265°). With the rate of closure at that angle down to 235 yards per minute, it would take another 10 minutes (or until 0553) for the range to close to 25,000 yards.

At about 0549, 12 minutes after the *Bismarck* and *Prinz Eugen* were first sighted, the range had closed to nearly 26,000 yards and Holland was getting close to giving the order to open fire on the German ships. He realised the vulnerability of the *Hood* to plunging fire at long ranges, so he wanted to pass through the critical zone of vulnerability as fast as possible. He therefore gave the order for his squadron to make a 20° turn to starboard on a new course of 300° towards the enemy.

Before the last 20° turn to starboard executed at 0549, the German ships were at a bearing of about 40° to the course of the British force. Now they were at a bearing of only 20° or so, making it impossible for the rear turrets of the British ships to bear on the enemy. With a traversing arc of 270–280°, the rear turrets could only turn to an angle of 40–45° from the centreline of the ship as

Enemy in Sight

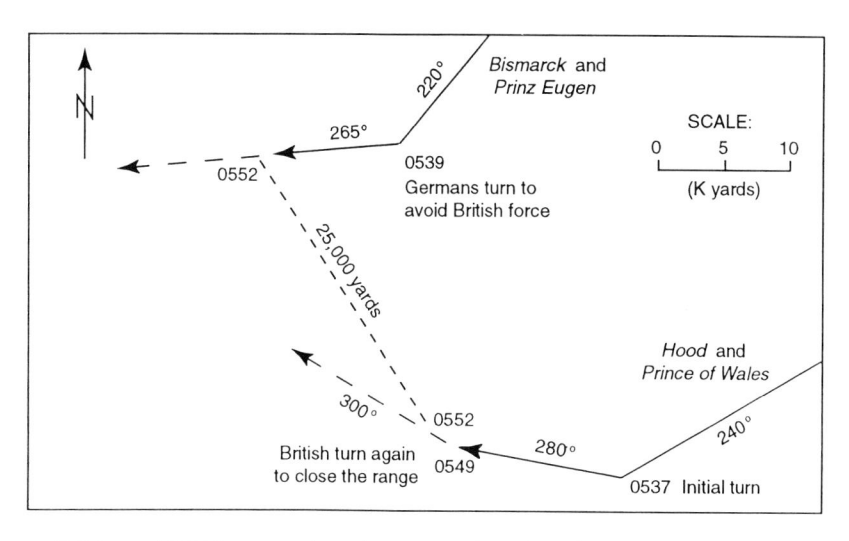

7-3 Second British turn to close the range to 25,000 yards by 0552.

measured from the bow in either direction. This meant that the British could engage the enemy with only half their total firepower.

The new angle of convergence of 35° increased the rate of closure to about 540 yards per minute. In another 3 minutes, the range would be down to 25,000 yards, and Admiral Holland could give the order to fire. The crews aboard the *Hood* and *Prince of Wales* were ready at their battle stations anxiously awaiting the word to engage the enemy.

The German squadron was also sailing into an uncertain situation. With the British force closing in on them, any thought about being able to elude the enemy was becoming increasingly doubtful. They were still not able to positively identify the British ships, but based on their speed, the possibility that they might be older battleships that could be easily outmanoeuvred rapidly disappeared. The Germans were still clinging to the belief that the British ships were two additional cruisers sent to reinforce the ones that had been trailing the German squadron during the night, but even this dream was slowly evaporating. As the British ships came closer, it also seemed unlikely that cruisers would deliberately close the range with a battleship.

CHAPTER 8

Open Fire

The two forces continued to close on each other, the British determined to stop the advance of the *Bismarck* into the North Atlantic and the Germans just as determined to achieve their objective. The sharp angle of approach by the British would not allow the rear turrets of the *Hood* and *Prince of Wales* to bear on the enemy ships, but the Germans had a similar problem. The *Bismarck* and *Prinz Eugen* were also sailing at a relatively steep angle in relation to the British force, and their forward turrets would be near their extreme limits for traversing towards the rear.

As the moment to open fire approached, the 15in guns of the forward turrets of the *Hood* were raised to an elevation of about 22°, which would give the projectiles the necessary range of 25,000 yards. Since the 14in guns of the *Prince of Wales* had somewhat different ballistic characteristics than the 15in guns of the *Hood*, her guns were elevated to a slightly lower angle, *ie* about 20°, to achieve the same range. The actual elevation of the guns with respect to each ship were then continuously adjusted to compensate for the rolling and pitching of the ship up to the time of firing. This ensured accurate gun-laying regardless of the attitude of the ship.

At 0552, the range had reached 25,000 yards, and Admiral Holland gave the order to open fire. In that order, he specified the lead ship as the target. In a few moments, the four 15in guns in the forward turrets of the *Hood* belched fire and smoke as each gun hurled an armour-piercing projectile weighing nearly a ton towards her designated target. At that range, it would take about 50 seconds for the shells to reach their target. The gunners could then observe the results of their fire by the splashes made by the shells as they exploded in the sea and make the necessary corrections before firing the next salvo.

Open Fire

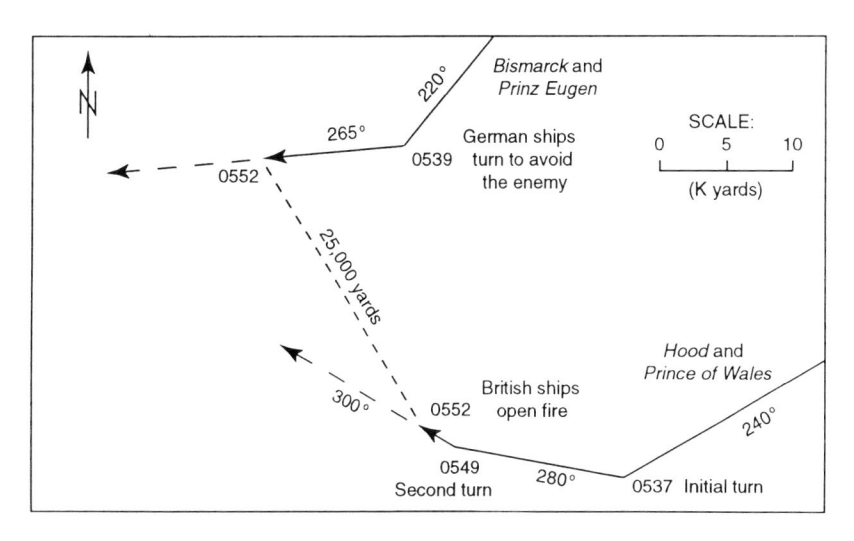

8–1 Position of British and German forces at the time the British opened fire.

The last part of Holland's order, designating the lead ship as the target, caused Captain Leach on the *Prince of Wales* some consternation. His Chief Gunnery Officer had already identified the rear ship as being the *Bismarck*. He decided to ignore the order from the flagship and take the word of his own expert as to the proper identification of the German ships. Leach must have been aware of the chance he was taking. If his gunnery officer were wrong, he would be endangering the British force by not engaging the ship that posed the greatest threat. In addition to the tactical considerations, there were personal consequences for failing to comply with a direct order from a superior in a combat situation. Such an act could lead to a court-martial and being cashiered out of the service, if not worse. On the other hand, he had total confidence in the ability of his gunnery officer and was personally satisfied that he was taking the correct action. There is no indication that Captain Leach ever made any attempt to contact the flagship regarding the action he was taking or to advise Admiral Holland of his belief that the German ships had not been correctly identified.

A few moments after the flagship fired, the forward turrets of the *Prince of Wales* roared in anger as six 14in guns let loose their projectiles weighing about 1600 pounds each at what her gunners

8–2 HMS *Hood* opening fire on the German squadron.

believed to be the *Bismarck*. Her shells would reach the target in about 45 seconds, 5 seconds faster than those of the *Hood*. Leach delayed firing after the flagship until there would be no chance of Hood's spotters mistaking *Prince of Wales'* fall of shot for their own. This precaution was actually academic since each ship was firing at a different target, but Leach was hoping that the gunners on the *Hood* would realise their error and shift their fire to the correct target.

Huge columns of water erupted around the *Prinz Eugen* as the *Hood's* first salvo arrived. A few seconds later, the *Bismarck* had a similar experience as *Prince of Wales'* shells landed near her. This finally ended any uncertainty as to the type of British ships approaching. Only the heavy guns of capital ships could produce the blasts seen as the British ships opened fire on the German squadron, and create the gigantic water spouts caused by their shells exploding in the sea. Their angle of approach still made it difficult to see any distinguishing features of the British ships and therefore they could still not be positively identified.

Lütjens was surprised that the *Prinz Eugen* was also coming under fire from the British ships, but not nearly as much as her crew were! A single heavy-calibre shell could wreak havoc upon their relatively lightly-armoured ship. A 15in shell was about 7½ times

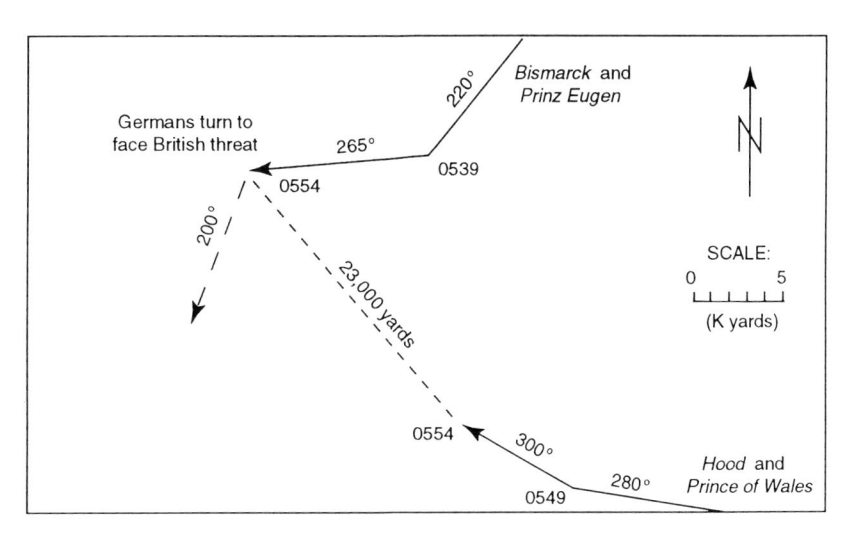

8–5 Position of British and German forces at the time of the German turn to face the British threat.

closure to more than 1000 yards per minute. In 4 minutes, the range would be 20,000 yards, and in 5 more minutes, there would be only 15,000 yards separating the British and German forces. The German ships were now on a course that was almost perpendicular to that of the approaching British and were in a position to 'cross their T'. They had therefore gained the tactical advantage of employing their full firepower while the British ships were limited to their forward turrets only, stripping them of their numerical superiority. The British were further handicapped by the technical problems suffered by the main armament of the *Prince of Wales*. After the initial salvo, one of the guns in the forward quadruple turret broke down, leaving her with only five 14in guns to fight with. Theoretically, this would have had put the two forces on a par with respect to major-calibre weapons. However, with the *Prinz Eugen* not otherwise engaged, she could add her firepower to the German side.

The *Prinz Eugen* opened fire first with all eight of her 8in guns at about 0553, soon after completing her turn and settling down on her new course. With her fast-firing guns, the *Prinz Eugen* could discharge four salvos a minute, and she began a blistering attack on the lead ship in the British force, the *Hood*. Her guns had a muzzle velocity of over 3000ft per second (nearly 25 per cent greater than the British 15in gun), and could cause considerable damage to lightly-armoured sections of her target. At the time the *Prinz Eugen* opened fire, the range was down to 23,000 yards, and it would take only 40 seconds before the results of her first salvo would be known. After the splashes were observed, the necessary corrections were made and rapid fire began.

The *Prinz Eugen* soon scored a hit on the starboard side of her target. The shell landed at one of the ammunition lockers amidships on the upper deck of the *Hood* and set the ammunition alight. This consisted of ready rounds for the twin 4in anti-aircraft guns mounted on that deck as well as ammunition for the unrifled projectile launchers (UPs) intended for defence against enemy aircraft. The UPs fired small bombs at attacking aircraft, which deployed by parachute directly in their path. Contact with any of the wires hanging down from the UPs would detonate the explosive charge carried in the device and thereby destroy the aircraft. Attempts to put out the fire were prevented by exploding ammunition. While not a fatal hit, it was nevertheless serious enough to cause some interference with the operation of the ship.

The British ships continued to fire at their respective targets, but without scoring any hits. By dividing their firepower between two separate targets, the British were actually reducing the odds of scoring a hit on either. It would only be a matter of time before the *Bismarck* herself would join in the firefight, and that was not a pleasant prospect.

CHAPTER 9

The Loss of HMS *Hood*

It was now the *Bismarck*'s turn to engage the enemy. She settled down after her turn to port, and once her gunners had worked out the initial firing solution, she opened fire at about 0555 with a full broadside of her eight 15in guns at the lead ship. At that time the range was down to 22,000 yards, and with her guns having a muzzle velocity of 2690ft per second and elevation of 13°, her 1760lb armour-piercing projectiles would reach their target in about 34 seconds. The shells fell close to the *Hood*, but no hits were observed. The gunners made the necessary adjustments to their aim, and the *Bismarck* fired again. Then there was another wait of 32 seconds before the tell-tale splashes would reveal the next fall of shot.

The *Hood* had fired at least two salvos at the *Prinz Eugen* before the German ships had made their turn to port. With both enemy ships now broadside-on, the gunners aboard the *Hood* could more readily distinguish the longer hull and other features that set the *Bismarck* apart from her consort and correctly identify their opponents. It is also possible that the *Hood*'s gunners had noticed that the *Prince of Wales* was directing her fire at the rear ship, and took a closer look at their respective targets to make sure that they were firing at the correct ship. In any event, they finally realised that they had been firing at the *Prinz Eugen* by mistake.

When the previous misidentification of the German ships was reported to Admiral Holland, he immediately signalled the *Prince of Wales* to shift targets to the second ship. Since Captain Leach had already been firing at the correct target, he ignored this order as he did the original order. Leach was relieved that the 'sticky' situation he had been in was satisfactorily resolved without any further ado. He could now devote his full attention to attempting to stop the

9-1 *Bismarck* fires on the *Hood* while far astern of *Prinz Eugen* (0556). (Photographer: Lagemann. Bundesarchiv: 68/15/24)

Bismarck, and not have to worry about the flagship firing at the wrong target and whether he should do anything about it.

Admiral Holland realised that the 65° turn to port by the Germans meant he was in imminent danger of 'having his T crossed' himself. While he was still anxious to sail through the zone of high vulnerability to plunging fire as fast as possible, he could not afford to lose his lead angle against the German squadron. He therefore ordered the British force to make a 20° turn to port, returning it to its previous course of 280°. This turn was executed at 0555, just about the same time that the *Hood* was hit by gunfire from the *Prinz Eugen*.

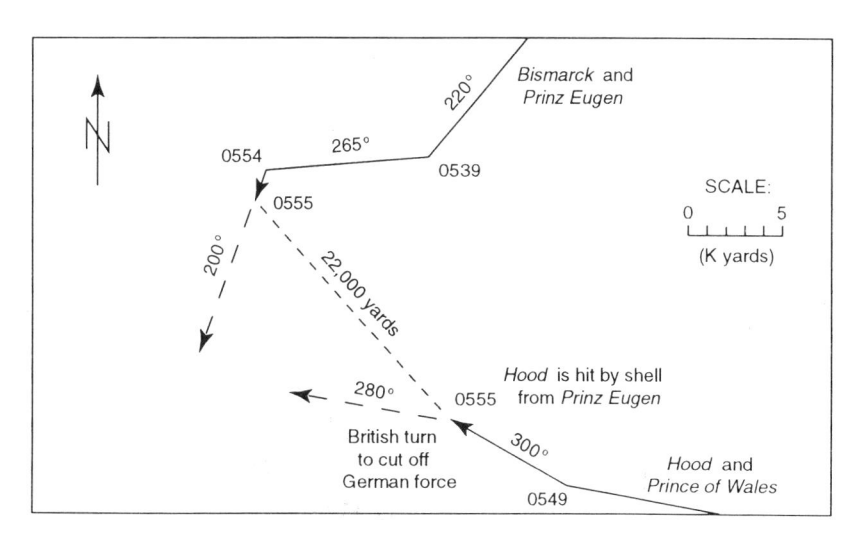

9–2 Position of British and German forces at the time of the first British turn to port.

The last turn to port by the British still placed them at an acute angle of approach to the Germans and precluded the use of their rear turrets. It did, however, put them in a better position to intercept the enemy squadron and keep it from taking the lead. With their slightly superior speed, especially over the *Prince of Wales*, the *Bismarck* and *Prinz Eugen* could have eventually pulled away from the British force if Holland had not taken this action.

Besides the handicap of being able to use only half of his available firepower, Holland had now placed his ships in the precarious position of sailing on a diagonal course across the enemy's line of fire. This exposed his ships to the greatest probability of a hit from each salvo that straddled the ship. Since the fall of shot would be elongated along the line of fire, more projectiles from each salvo would have a chance of hitting the ship (see Appendix A). Furthermore, the German ships were almost perpendicular to the British line of fire, thereby reducing the probability of a hit across the elongated pattern of fall of shot.

The Germans believed that they had finally identified their adversaries as the *Hood* and *King George V*. The error of mistaking the *Prince of Wales* for the *King George V* was perfectly natural since the *Prince of Wales* was virtually identical in overall appearance to her sister-ship, and she was thought to be still not ready for service. Lütjens was perplexed by the sudden appearance of what he believed to be the two most powerful ships in the Royal Navy, which were thought to be still at Scapa Flow. He at last realised that the British had been fully aware of his sortie and that this was not merely a chance encounter.

The *Prinz Eugen* continued her rapid fire against the *Hood*, but achieved no further hits on her adversary. The *Bismarck* achieved a straddle on the *Hood* with her third salvo, and Lütjens knew that it

9-3 *Bismarck* continues to fire on the *Hood* as she moves up to take the lead (0558). (Photographer: Lagemann. Bundesarchiv: 90/61/27).

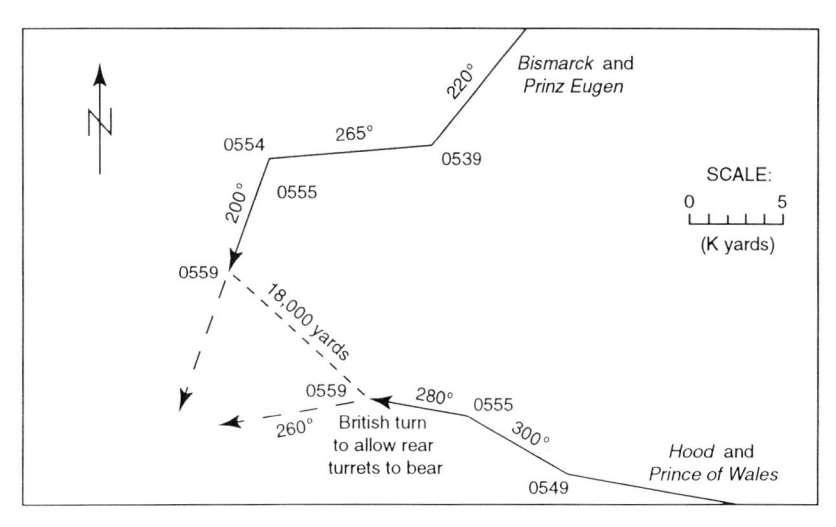

9-4 British turn another 20° to port to allow their rear turrets to bear upon the enemy.

was just a matter of time before she would begin scoring hits. Not wanting to leave the *Prince of Wales* unengaged, Lütjens ordered the *Prinz Eugen* to shift targets to her. He further ordered the *Prinz Eugen* to drop back off the starboard side of the *Bismarck* and take position to the rear. There she could keep the British cruisers *Norfolk* and *Suffolk*, still trailing the German force, under observation and prevent any unexpected incursion from that direction.

By this time, the British ships had fired several salvos from their forward turrets, without effect. The probability of scoring a hit with only four or five guns was far less than with full eight- to nine-gun broadsides. It was therefore necessary for the British ships to turn parallel to the enemy so that they could bring all of their guns into play against the *Bismarck* as soon as possible, even though it would subject the *Hood* to plunging fire for a little while longer. Holland accepted this risk and ordered his force to make another 20° turn to port on a new course of 260°. This turn was executed at about 0559, and it put the German ships at a bearing of about 55°, finally allowing the British ships to bring their full armament to bear.

The second salvo by the *Bismarck* also missed the *Hood*, but by then her gunners had realised that the British ships had made a slight turn from their previous course. They waited until the new

The Bismarck Chase

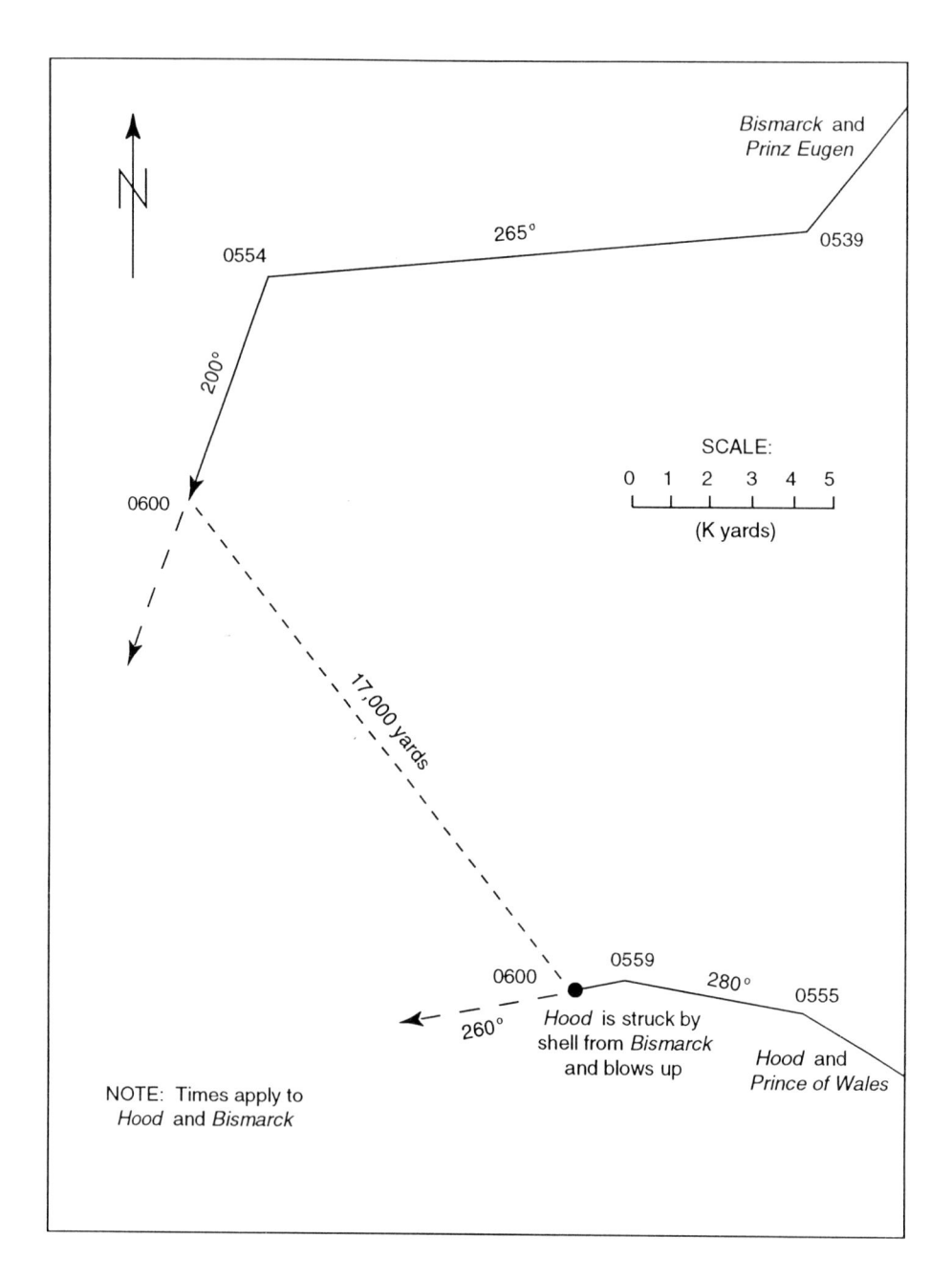

9–5 Position of British and German forces when HMS *Hood* was hit by shell from the *Bismarck*.

The Loss of HMS Hood

9–7 A huge column of smoke rises from the stricken *Hood*, as seen from the *Prinz Eugen*. (Photographer: Lagemann. Bundesarchiv: 98/34/5)

taking a gradual list to port. A look outside by one of the crewmembers revealed the stern obscured by smoke and confirmed the fact the ship was indeed sinking.

The blown-off aft section of the *Hood* quickly slowed down as its ragged broad surface, acting as a brake, pushed against the sea and rapidly filled with water. It gradually tilted forward as the water gushed in, lifting the stern completely out of the water and exposing the ship's screws and rudder. In less than a minute, the stern slipped beneath the sea, taking all within it to a watery grave.

The fore section, on the other hand, continued to surge ahead with the momentum imparted to its remaining 30,000 tons of steel.

The Bismarck Chase

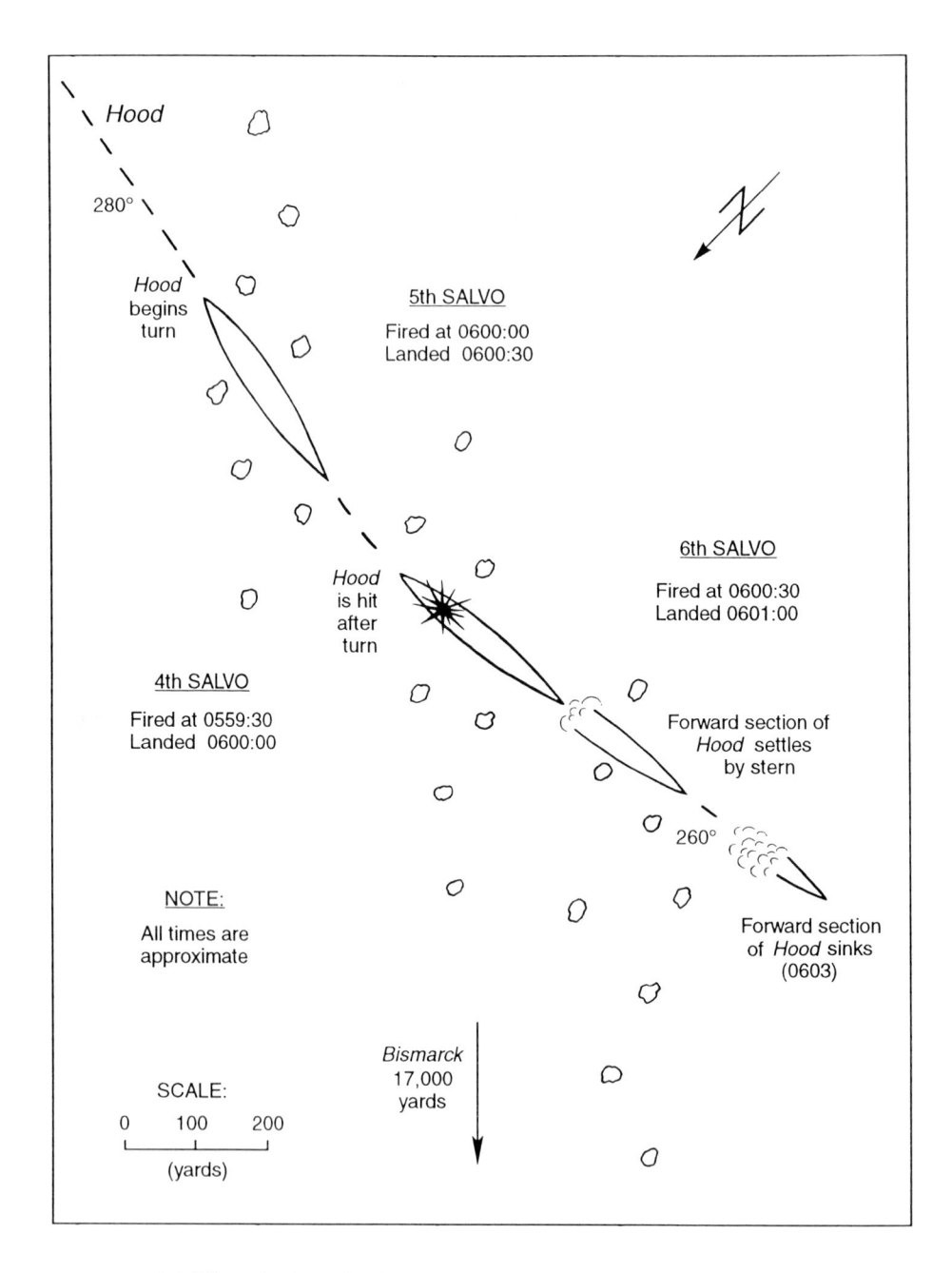

Hood

280°

Hood begins turn

5th SALVO

Fired at 0600:00
Landed 0600:30

Hood is hit after turn

6th SALVO

Fired at 0600:30
Landed 0601:00

4th SALVO

Fired at 0559:30
Landed 0600:00

Forward section of *Hood* settles by stern

260°

Forward section of *Hood* sinks (0603)

NOTE:

All times are approximate

Bismarck 17,000 yards

SCALE:
0   100   200
(yards)

9–8 Effect of salvoes fired at HMS *Hood* by *Bismarck*.

Without the push from the engines and screws, the fore section also began to slow down and take on water through its shattered rear end, and the bow began to rise in the air. Crew members who were on the bridge and nearby positions on deck, or otherwise had access to avenues of escape, began to scramble for survival as the ship took on a greater list and sank deeper into the water.

The sea finally closed over her bow about 3 minutes after the *Hood* had been struck, taking hundred of men to the ocean floor. For a few moments, the sea seamed to boil as the air trapped in the sinking ship bubbled its way to the surface. All that remained were pieces of floating debris, patches of fuel oil, a few Carley floats, and a handful of survivors.

There had been little time to abandon ship once it was obvious the *Hood* was going to sink, but several crewmen were able to get clear of the ship before she went down. Admiral Holland and Captain Kerr apparently made no effort to escape and went down with their ship in true naval tradition. Thus ended the illustrious career of the most revered ship in the Royal Navy and one of the most famous warships of the twentieth century. Admiral Wake-Walker, who saw the *Hood* blow up from the bridge of the *Norfolk*, immediately radioed the news to the Admiralty and to Admiral Tovey on *King George V* which was still sailing west to intercept the *Bismarck*.

CHAPTER 10

HMS *Prince of Wales* Fights Alone

The *Hood* was gone, but the battle was not over yet. When the *Prince of Wales* had completed the last 20° turn to port at 0600, she was approximately 1000 yards directly astern of the *Hood*. Seeing the flagship explode ahead of him, Captain Leach ordered a hard turn to starboard to avoid hitting the wreckage. This manoeuvre turned the *Prince of Wales* toward the *Bismarck* and closed the arc of his rear turret so that it could no longer bear. As soon as her guns could be retrained on the *Bismarck*, she fired another salvo with the functioning guns of her forward turrets.

The *Prince of Wales* soon came up alongside the stricken flagship engulfed in a cloud of smoke. Through the smoke, Captain Leach could see the stern still above water, but sinking, and the forward section still with some forward momentum but listing to port and filling rapidly. After clearing the remains of the *Hood*, Leach swung back to a course of 260°, which again brought his ship's full broadside to bear. She was sailing on a diagonal course towards the *Bismarck* with the range continuing to drop, and this put her in a very vulnerable position. At shorter ranges, the pattern of fall of shot is narrower and more elongated, increasing the odds for a hit with a well-aimed salvo.

At about 0602, the *Prince of Wales* had settled on her new course and resumed fire. When the *Hood* blew up, the crews of the *Bismarck* and *Prinz Eugen* were at first struck with awe and then overcome with jubilation. They had just destroyed the pride of the Royal Navy without receiving any damage in return. This was truly remarkable and tended to confirm their earlier beliefs of invincibility. But they soon realised that they still faced a dangerous opponent capable of doing them serious harm.

HMS *Prince of Wales* Fights Alone

Bismarck and
Prinz Eugen

200°

N

SCALE:
0 1 2 3 4 5
(K yards)

0603 *Prinz Eugen* holds fire
as *Bismarck* passes

15,000 yards

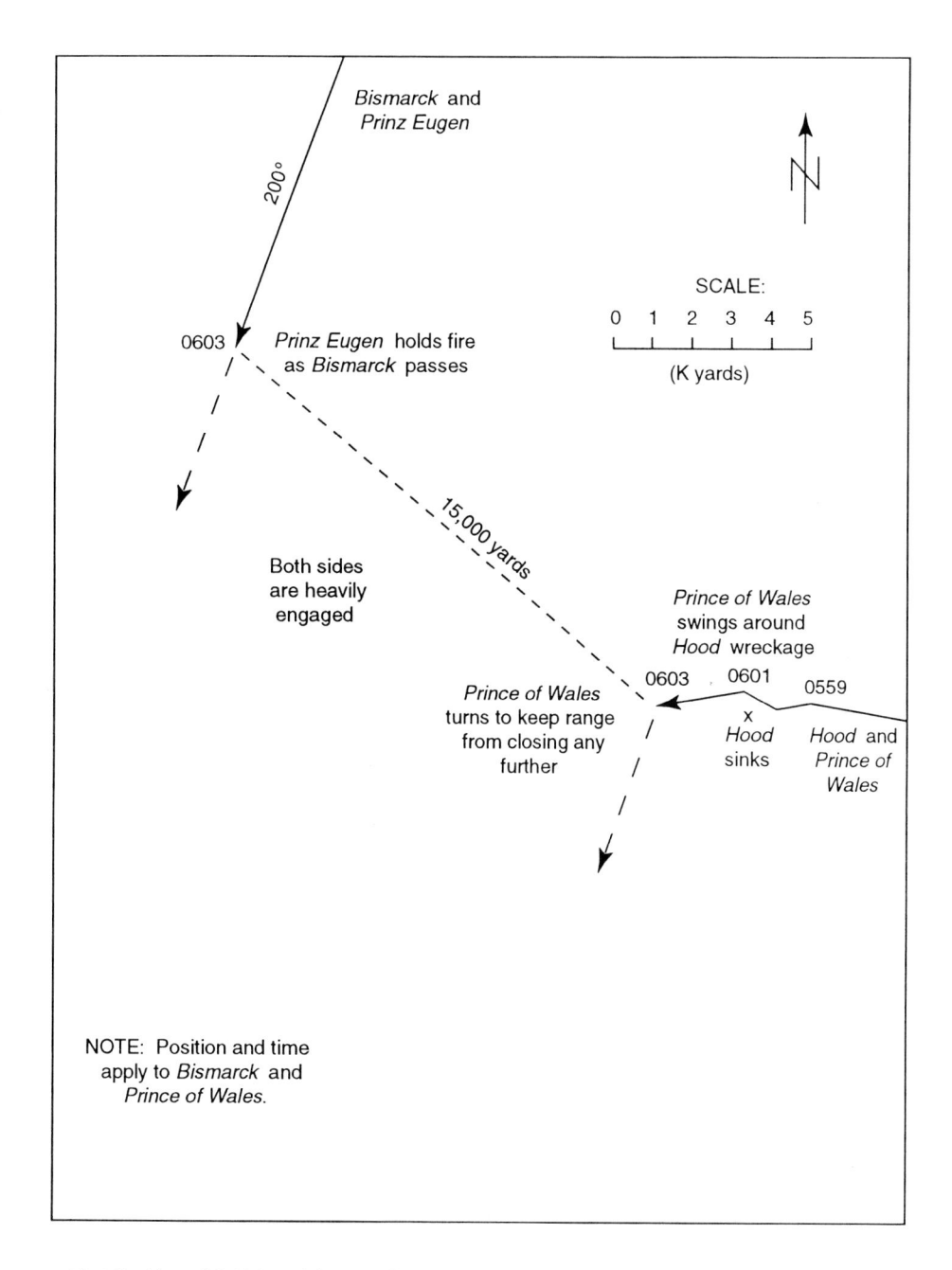

Both sides
are heavily
engaged

Prince of Wales
swings around
Hood wreckage

Prince of Wales
turns to keep range
from closing any
further

0603   0601   0559
       X
       Hood   *Hood* and
       sinks   *Prince of
                   Wales*

NOTE: Position and time
apply to *Bismarck* and
Prince of Wales.

10–1 Position of British and German forces when HMS *Prince of Wales* turned to prevent range closing further.

10–2 *Bismarck* pulls ahead of *Prinz Eugen* as she continues to fire on *Prince of Wales*. (Photographer: Lagemann. Bundesarchiv: 85/24/12)

Once the gunners on the *Bismarck* had recovered themselves, they turned their attention to the *Prince of Wales*. This was relatively easy, since she was now at approximately the same range as *Hood* had been when she was hit and only a degree or two to the left. The *Prinz Eugen* had already been firing on the *Prince of Wales*, in compliance with the earlier order from Lütjens, and she was beginning to zero in on her target. The turns by the *Prince of Wales* to get around the wreckage of the *Hood* momentarily disrupted the gunnery of the *Bismarck* and *Prinz Eugen*, but as she returned to her prior course, the gunners on the German ships worked out their gunnery solutions.

The two German ships then jointly opened a withering fire against the *Prince of Wales*, pumping out armour-piercing projectiles as fast as their guns could be reloaded. By 0603, the range had come down to 15,000 yards and the exchange of gunfire was beginning to have a serious effect on both sides. At that range, there was a good chance of achieving a hit with every salvo and it was taking only 20 seconds for the shells to reach their targets. A 15in shell from the *Bismarck* soon hit the bridge of the *Prince of Wales*, with devastating results. Although the shell passed through the bridge without exploding, it killed several key personnel on the bridge and momentarily stunned Captain Leach. That hit had, at least temporarily, disrupted command of the *Prince of Wales*, and direction of operations had to be transferred to the aft control position of the ship.

An 8in shell from the *Prinz Eugen* then hit the base of the forward fire control director for the secondary armament. That hit knocked out the control functions for several of the 5.25in guns on the ship, and those functions had to be transferred to the rear director. She soon scored two more hits on the *Prince of Wales* with a single salvo. Those hits were below the waterline in the stern. Damage was not extensive, but the hits did cause some flooding that had to be balanced by counter-flooding. About to be overtaken by the *Bismarck* passing off her port beam, the *Prinz Eugen* had to cease fire at about 0603 and would not be able to fire again for another couple of minutes.

Leach, not wanting to reduce the range any further, ordered his ship to execute a sharp turn to port at about 0603. That turn would maintain the present range and place the *Prince of Wales* on a course nearly parallel to that of the German squadron. She continued to fire at the *Bismarck* and was obviously scoring straddles, but no hits were observed. During this phase of the battle, the *Prince of Wales* did actually score three hits on the *Bismarck*, but they were not seen and had no apparent effect on her fighting capability. The *Prinz Eugen* was in a very vulnerable position as the *Bismarck* passed her since she was in the direct line of fire from the *Prince of Wales*. Any salvoes over the *Bismarck* had a good chance of hitting her while in that situation.

The *Bismarck* scored again with a 15in shell that first struck the starboard crane and then exploded abaft the rear funnel of the *Prince of Wales*. That hit did extensive splinter damage to the superstructure, compartments, Walrus aircraft on the catapult between the two funnels, boats, and other exposed equipment. Another shell hit amidships under the rear funnel far below the waterline, but fortunately failed to explode. This caused some flooding and loss of fuel oil, which adversely affected the speed and endurance of the ship.

After another minute of exchanging heavy fire, Leach took stock of the situation. By that time, his ship had already received four hits

10-3 *Bismarck* receives fire from *Prince of Wales* while *Prinz Eugen* falls back (0605). (Photographer: Lagemann. Bundesarchiv: 68/15/12)

10–4 Smoke from rapid-fire salvoes trails the *Bismarck* as a shell from *Prince of Wales* lands close by (0606). (Photographer: Lagemann. Bundesarchiv: 90/81/10A)

by heavy-calibre shells from the *Bismarck* in addition to the three 8in hits scored by the *Prinz Eugen*. Difficulties were still being experienced with the main armament, making it impossible to keep up effective fire. The damage done to the *Prince of Wales*, while not critical, had an adverse effect on the execution of further combat operations, and his crew lacked sufficient experience to compensate properly.

In the exchange of gunfire, the *Prince of Wales* was definitely getting the worst of it by far, with little visible damage having been

The Bismarck Chase

10-5 *Bismarck* continuing to fire at *Prince of Wales* which is retiring behind a smokescreen (0607). (Photographer: Lagemann. Bundesarchiv: 68/15/26)

inflicted on the *Bismarck*. Believing that further engagement could possibly result in more serious damage and possible loss of his ship without any corresponding impact on the enemy, Captain Leach ordered the *Prince of Wales* to withdraw behind a smoke screen. It was a difficult decision to make, but he felt that he had no other choice. He knew that there were other ships on the way to intercept the *Bismarck*, and he considered it foolhardy to risk a valuable asset of the Royal Navy for what seemed now a remote possibility of inflicting some damage to the enemy.

Whether it had any influence on Leach's decision to disengage is

HMS *Prince of Wales* Fights Alone

uncertain, but there was another factor that could have contributed to the plight of the *Prince of Wales*. The *Bismarck* had just completed passing her cruiser consort, leaving the *Prinz Eugen* free to resume firing. She had already scored three hits on the *Prince of Wales*, and with her rapid-firing 8in guns, she could throw over a ton of explosives at the British ship every 15 seconds. While these shells could not inflict any mortal damage on her heavily-armoured adversary, they could affect her overall combat efficiency in many ways, such as disabling her exposed fire-control instruments and causing heavy casualties in her more lightly-armoured spaces.

10–6 *Bismarck* firing on the retiring *Prince of Wales* (0608). (Photographer: Lagemann. Bundesarchiv: 68/15/22)

The Bismarck Chase

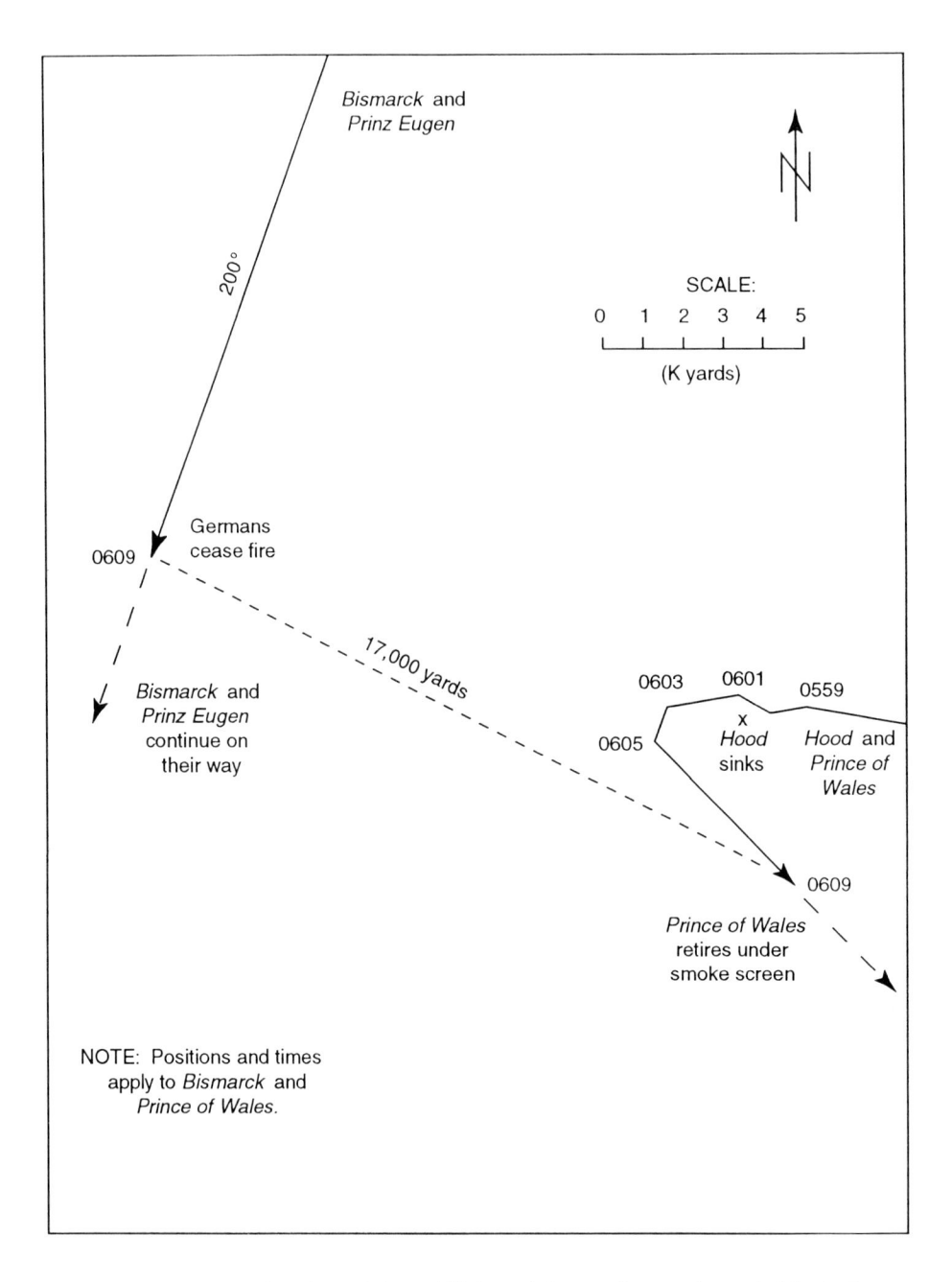

10–7 Position of HMS *Prince of Wales* and German force at the end of the battle.

Before his turn-away, Leach radioed his intentions to Rear-Admiral Wake-Walker aboard the *Norfolk*, still trailing the German squadron. With the loss of Admiral Holland on the *Hood*, Wake-Walker automatically became the senior officer present. Leach knew that the admiral was actually several miles away and could not have a true appreciation of the situation, but he had to follow naval protocol, and Wake-Walker concurred with his decision.

At about 0605, the *Prince of Wales* turned to the south-east on a new course of about 150°, making smoke to conceal her movements. She continued firing at the *Bismarck* with her rear turret, but this was just harassing fire which was not expected to have any effect except to keep the *Bismarck* at bay. The gunners were also hindered by the smoke being created by their own ship and could only aim blindly along the course that the enemy was following. The *Bismarck* continued to fire in the direction of the smoke and at the estimated range of the *Prince of Wales*, but Lütjens did not expect any further hits under those circumstances. At about 0609, both sides decided not to waste any more ammunition and ceased firing.

Admiral Lütjens was somewhat surprised to see the *Prince of Wales* turn away from the action and retire behind a smoke screen. He knew that both the *Prinz Eugen* and the *Bismarck* had scored several hits on her, but he had no idea of the damage that had been done. Some officers aboard the *Bismarck* expressed the view that they should pursue the *Prince of Wales* and 'finish her off,' but that of course was out of the question.

Lütjens realised that to pursue the *Prince of Wales* would be contrary to his standing orders to avoid any engagement with enemy naval units except those defending Allied convoys. While she was undoubtedly damaged, there seemed to be little impact on her firepower and speed, and she was therefore still capable of inflicting serious damage on the *Bismarck*. He also had to consider that any pursuit could lead the German squadron closer to other British naval units that were undoubtedly on their way to intercept the *Bismarck*.

There was also the condition of the *Bismarck* herself. She had sustained three hits from 14in shells from *Prince of Wales*. Two of those hits were not significant and caused only superficial damage,

The Bismarck Chase

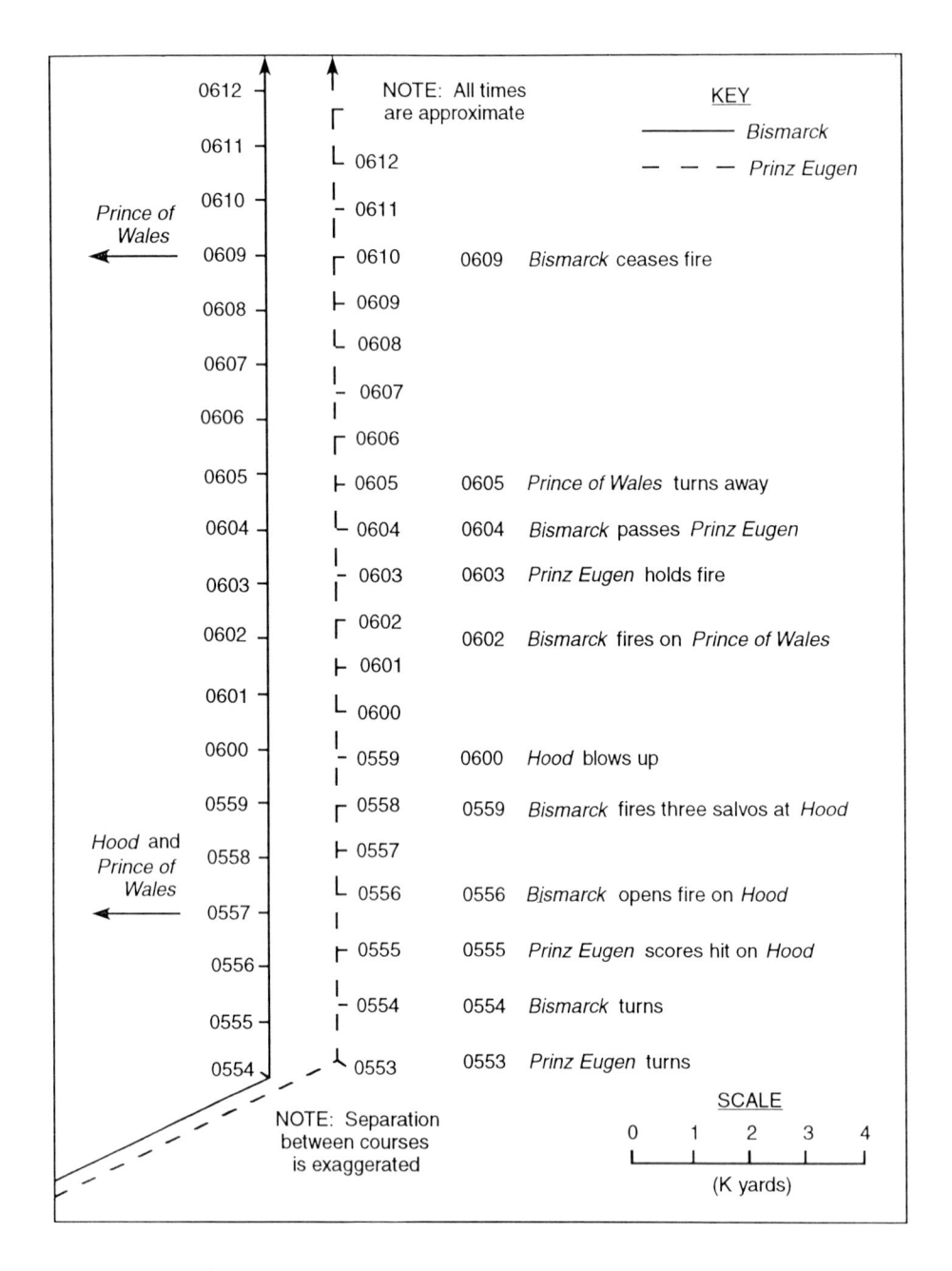

```
                    NOTE: All times                    KEY
    0612              are approximate
                    ┌                           ─────────── Bismarck
    0611            └ 0612
                    │                           ─ ─ ─ ─    Prinz Eugen
    0610            ┌ 0611
Prince of           │
Wales   0609        ┌ 0610      0609  Bismarck ceases fire
◄────
        0608        ├ 0609
                    └ 0608
        0607        │
                    ├ 0607
        0606        │
                    ┌ 0606
        0605        ├ 0605      0605  Prince of Wales turns away
        0604        └ 0604      0604  Bismarck passes Prinz Eugen
                    │
        0603        ├ 0603      0603  Prinz Eugen holds fire
                    │
        0602        ┌ 0602      0602  Bismarck fires on Prince of Wales
                    ├ 0601
        0601        │
                    └ 0600
        0600        │
                    ├ 0559      0600  Hood blows up
                    │
        0559        ┌ 0558      0559  Bismarck fires three salvos at Hood
Hood and            ├ 0557
Prince of 0558
Wales               └ 0556      0556  Bismarck opens fire on Hood
        0557        │
◄────               ┌ 0555      0555  Prinz Eugen scores hit on Hood
        0556        │
                    ├ 0554      0554  Bismarck turns
        0555        │
        0554        ↓ 0553      0553  Prinz Eugen turns
                                             SCALE
                    NOTE: Separation      0   1   2   3   4
                    between courses       └───┴───┴───┴───┘
                    is exaggerated              (K yards)
```

10-8 Tracks of *Bismarck* and *Prinz Eugen* during battle with *Hood* and *Prince of Wales*.

but the third hit was far more serious. The shell had struck below the waterline in the forward part of the hull, causing some flooding and reducing the top speed of the ship. It would have therefore been difficult to keep up with the *Prince of Wales*, let alone finish her off. In addition to the flooding problem, that hit had also ruptured several fuel tanks, causing the loss of much of the *Bismarck*'s precious fuel reserves and leaving a conspicuous trail of oil behind the ship.

Figure 10–9 shows the relative tracks of the British and German forces from the time of initial sighting to the end of the battle. In several previous publications, the German force was reported as following a straight-line course of about 220° throughout the battle rather than the two large turns described in this book. That straight-line course is shown in Figure 10–9 for purposes of comparison with the more accurate track of the German force described in this book. The straight-line track appears to be consistent in timing with the position of the German force with respect to its direction, but the ranges do not correspond to the known distances between the two opposing forces during the battle.

Only the turns described herein meet all of the parameters associated with the relative tracks of the British and German forces. If the German squadron had maintained its original course of 220° throughout the engagement, they would have been within effective firing range of 25,000 yards in only 6 minutes (or by 0543). By the time the British did open fire 15 minutes after the first sighting (at 0552), the straight-line course by the Germans would have brought the range down to only 17,000 yards instead of 25,000 yards. At 0603, when the *Bismarck* was engaging the *Prince of Wales*, the range was reported down to 15,000 yards, but a steady course of 220° would have placed the Germans only 10,000 yards away at that time.

Logic also tends to support the description of the German track as contained in this book. It would make no sense for Lütjens to keep on a straight course that was converging with an enemy force of unknown strength when he had other options available. As described earlier, there was the possibility that the British ships could have been older battleships which the German squadron could

The Bismarck Chase

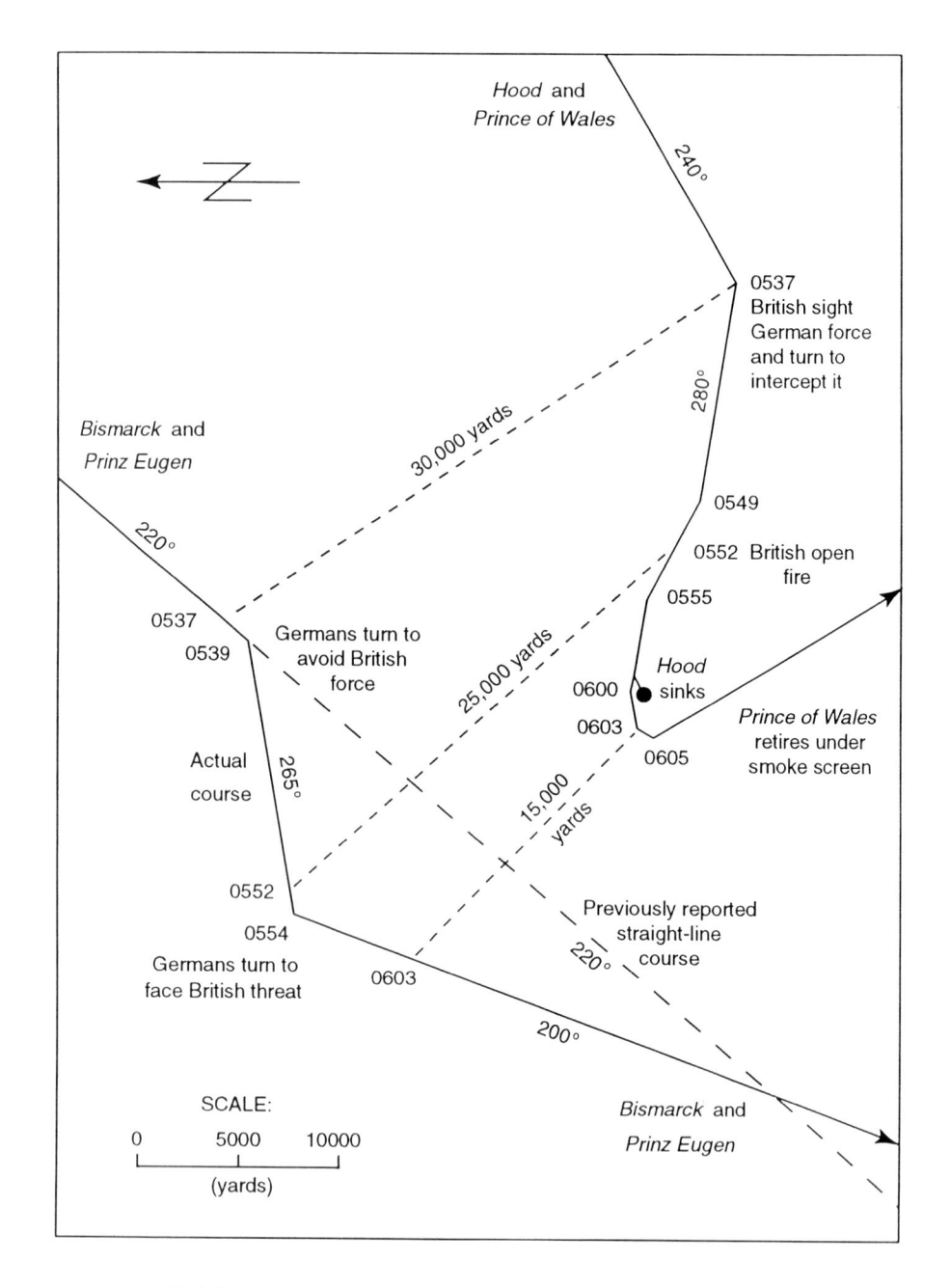

10–9 Relative tracks of British and German forces during the battle.

easily outrun and circle around. In any event, the first turn away from the British force allowed Lütjens more time to positively identify this new threat and to develop a strategy for meeting it. The second turn was also necessary so that the German ships could be placed across the path of the oncoming British ships for more effective broadside firing and also to reduce the odds for a hit by enemy fire.

There is another inconsistency in earlier publications that this book attempts to clarify. In numerous works, several of the photographs taken of the *Bismarck* from the *Prinz Eugen* during the latter phase of the battle appear to have been printed in reverse. They show the *Bismarck* firing to starboard, which is of course impossible since the enemy was always to port of her. The photographs also show the *Prinz Eugen* on different sides of the *Bismarck*, which is also inconsistent with the facts. These photographs, identified as Figures 10–1 through 10–6, are shown in their proper orientation in this book.

By carefully studying all of the photographs taken of the *Bismarck* from the *Prinz Eugen* during the battle, five conclusions can be drawn which tend to support the scenario of events as presented in this book:

- The *Prinz Eugen* had made a turn to port just before the German squadron opened fire, as evidenced by her curved wake as shown in Figure 9–1, which supports the conclusion of a second turn taken by the German force.

- The *Bismarck* followed a straight course while engaging the *Hood* and *Prince of Wales*, as evidenced by no indication of any turning or lateral movement in those photographs. This contradicts some earlier accounts of her taking evasive action to avoid torpedoes fired by the *Prince of Wales*, which, in any case, was not equipped with torpedo tubes.

- The *Bismarck* always kept the *Prinz Eugen* on her starboard side, where the cruiser would be protected against enemy fire. After the battle, the *Prinz Eugen* moved up, still on the starboard side of the *Bismarck*, to take the lead of the German squadron (Figures 11–1, 11–2 and 11–4).

- The *Bismarck* was firing in a direction nearly perpendicular to her line of travel as evidenced by the orientation of her turrets as shown in Figure 10–3. This supports the conclusion of a second turn and a course that brought the German squadron steaming across the path of the British force.
- Other photographs showing the *Bismarck* astern or ahead of the *Prinz Eugen* also reveal her guns aimed well to port, which further supports the above conclusion.

CHAPTER 11

Bismarck Escapes

Admiral Lütjens decided not to pursue the *Prince of Wales* but to proceed with his mission. He considered himself lucky to have come out of the battle against a superior force with so little damage, and he did not want to press his luck any further. The *Prinz Eugen* was again ordered to take the lead with her operational radar. The *Bismarck* slowed down so that she could come up on her starboard side and move ahead of her. It was now time to make a reassessment of the situation in view of the damage sustained to the *Bismarck*.

Lütjens soon realised that he could not continue with his mission without repair of the damage inflicted on his flagship. The ruptured fuel tanks would have a serious impact on the endurance of the ship and significantly reduce his range of operations. He therefore decided to detach the *Prinz Eugen* to proceed with raiding operations on her own, since she was still undamaged. As for the *Bismarck*, she would have to go to a port with a dry-dock of sufficient size to accommodate her. The closest one under German control was the huge dry-dock at the French port of St Nazaire on the Atlantic coast which had been built for the great French liner *Normandie*.

St Nazaire was the obvious choice, and it had certain longer-term possibilities. Repairs would not take long as the damage was not extensive. From St Nazaire, the *Bismarck* could link up with the battlecruisers *Gneisenau* and *Scharnhorst*, now at Brest, and form a more powerful battlegroup than with just the *Prinz Eugen*. That would bring Operation 'Rhine Exercise' closer to its original concept. In the meantime, the *Prinz Eugen* might be able to inflict some damage on British convoys by herself and keep the Royal Navy busy until the new battlegroup could be formed.

Once the action with the *Bismarck* had been broken off and the *Prince of Wales* was out of range of German guns, Captain Leach

The Bismarck Chase

11–1 *Bismarck* after breaking off action with *Prince of Wales*. (Photographer: Lagemann. Bundesarchiv: 68/15/31)

slowed his ship and turned to rendezvous with the *Suffolk* and *Norfolk*. The cruisers had continued to follow the German squadron after the *Hood* was sunk and the *Prince of Wales* disengaged. As soon as the *Norfolk* appeared, Leach conferred by signal with Admiral Wake-Walker. The Admiral had to continue the pursuit of the *Bismarck*, and he ordered the *Prince of Wales* to join his squadron in that pursuit regardless of the damage she had sustained. She was still a potent fighting machine that might yet be needed to help destroy the *Bismarck* in conjunction with other units of the Royal Navy en route to intercept the enemy.

With the status of the *Prince of Wales* settled and the pursuit renewed, Wake-Walker turned to other pressing matters, the most urgent of which was the rescue of survivors of the *Hood*. His cruisers passed the area where the *Hood* went down, but there was little that he could do about it under the circumstances. He could not afford to divert his force to pick up survivors and risk the possibility of losing the *Bismarck*. Admiral Wake-Walker was in charge of the operation and therefore the *Norfolk* could not be spared. The *Suffolk* had the better radar, so she also was essential to the pursuit. Therefore, neither of his cruisers could be spared for the humanitarian task of rescuing their comrades.

Wake-Walker ordered the six destroyers that had been escorting the *Hood* and *Prince of Wales* before they were detached by Admiral Holland due to rough seas to search for survivors from the *Hood*. It took the destroyers over an hour to reach the position where she had gone down, which was by then was covered by an assortment of floating debris and patches of oil. Amid the flotsam, HMS *Electra* could find only three survivors on Carley rafts out of the *Hood*'s complement of over 1420 officers and men. The destroyers continued to search the area where the *Hood* sank for more survivors, but they finally had to abandon the effort.

The destroyers then sailed to Hvalfjord, where the *Electra* landed the three men who had survived. It is possible that a few more crew members were able to get off the *Hood* alive in the 3 minutes that it took her to sink. There were crewmen on the bridge, in the radio room, at AA gun positions on deck, or in close proximity to exits from the forward superstructure of the ship who could have made their escape. If in fact any more had escaped from the ship, it is likely that they perished in the freezing water during the hour or more that it took the destroyers to reach the area.

Engineers and damage-control parties on the *Prince of Wales* quickly took stock of the damage that the ship had sustained. Debris was promptly removed, repairs within the scope of the crew were undertaken, and the *Prince of Wales* was soon made as shipshape as possible under the circumstances. The civilian technicians on board continued their work on the main armament system, which had given trouble throughout the engagement. They finally succeeded in restoring, at least temporarily, the full firepower of the ship. The *Prince of Wales* was again ready for action.

During the mid-afternoon of 24 May, the three-ship task force under Wake-Walker continued to maintain contact with the German

The Bismarck Chase

squadron, which was now steaming at high speed in a south-westerly direction. Shortly after noon, the German ships turned south and made desperate manoeuvres in attempts to shake off their pursuers. Lütjens had the *Bismarck* and *Prinz Eugen* slow down, suddenly speed up and change direction, and take other evasive action in an attempt to lose the British task force, but to no avail.

Wake-Walker was keeping the Admiralty appraised of the ongoing chase throughout the day. Based on that information, the Admiralty was orchestrating the convergence of all available British naval forces in the region toward the interception of the German squadron. The remainder of the Home Fleet under Admiral Tovey was now steaming in a south-westerly direction to link up with Wake-Walker in the pursuit of the *Bismarck*. The crews of his ships were eager to intercept the *Bismarck* and avenge the *Hood*.

In addition to the other ships already committed, the battleships *Rodney*, *Ramillies*, and *Revenge* and the cruisers *London* and *Edinburgh* were detached from convoy or patrol duty in the North Atlantic to aid in the search and destruction of the *Bismarck*. Force H at Gibraltar, under the command of Vice-Admiral Sir James Somerville was also alerted to participate in the chase should the *Bismarck* head in that direction. That force consisted of the battlecruiser *Renown* (sister-ship of the *Repulse*), the aircraft carrier *Ark Royal*, and the light cruiser *Sheffield*.

The morning of 24 May had remained relatively clear with only occasional small patches of fog. The British ships were therefore able to maintain not only radar contact, but also visual contact with the *Bismarck* for most of the morning. In the early afternoon, the weather began to deteriorate, and the German squadron became more difficult to see. Lütjens decided that this would be a good opportunity to detach the *Prinz Eugen*. His plan was to turn on his pursuers out of the fog with guns blazing and create enough of a diversion to allow the *Prinz Eugen* to escape undetected in the confusion. An earlier attempt in mid-afternoon had to be aborted when the *Bismarck* became visible too soon.

In the early evening, while both ships were in a fog bank, the *Bismarck* made a sudden 180° turn toward her pursuers. As she emerged from the fog bank, she opened fire on the following British

Bismarck Escapes

which would again put her out of radar contact with the *Bismarck* for a few moments. When the cruiser seemed to be approaching the limit of her south-eastward swing, Lütjens ordered the *Bismarck* to make an immediate turn to starboard and to continue almost due west at high speed away from the British force. The manoeuvre worked. When the *Suffolk* returned to the south-westward leg of her zigzag course, her radar did not pick up the *Bismarck* as it had done after earlier zigzags. Concentrating on the *Bismarck*, the *Suffolk* was not yet aware that the *Prinz Eugen* had already escaped.

When the loss of radar contact with the *Bismarck* was reported to Admiral Wake-Walker on the *Norfolk*, he immediately ordered his two cruisers to steam in a south-westerly and then a westerly direction in an attempt to regain it. Lütjens, however, instead of renewing his southerly course after breaking free, decided to make a wide swing to the north and circle around to the rear of the British ships. Once he had completed the circle, he headed in a south-easterly direction toward St Nazaire. By dawn, it became apparent that the *Bismarck* and *Prinz Eugen* had successfully eluded their pursuers and that it would take the combined resources of all available British air and sea forces to find them again.

CHAPTER 12

Bismarck is Discovered

The location and destination of the *Bismarck* became a matter of wide speculation among the British. If she had been heavily damaged by the *Prince of Wales*, would she double back and return to Germany? If she was only slightly damaged, would she head for the French coast for repairs or rendezvous with a naval auxiliary vessel to accomplish any necessary repairs at sea? Would she rendezvous with a tanker to take on more fuel? Would she immediately begin operations against convoys in the North Atlantic? The British did not have sufficient resources to adequately cover all of those possibilities, so it became a matter of assessing their probabilities and prioritising the allocation of resources to cover the various alternatives.

Admiral Tovey continued to sail in a south-westerly direction while the *Prince of Wales* was ordered to remain on a southerly course and join his task force. Force H, now more urgently required than before, was proceeding northward off Spain after leaving its convoy a few hours earlier. Other units of the Royal Navy were also converging on the area to assist in the search for the *Bismarck*. It seemed that the noose was tightening, but there was still a lot of ocean to hide in. Unknown to either side, the course of the *Bismarck*, after making her circle around Wake-Walker's force, cut across the track of Tovey's force after he had passed several hours before.

As soon as it became light enough on the morning of 25 May, the *Victorious* was ordered to make an air search to the north-west for the *Bismarck*, but by that time she was already south-east of that area and heading further away. Several Swordfish took off and after a search of several hours, they returned without success. One Swordfish did not return and was lost without trace.

Bismarck is Discovered

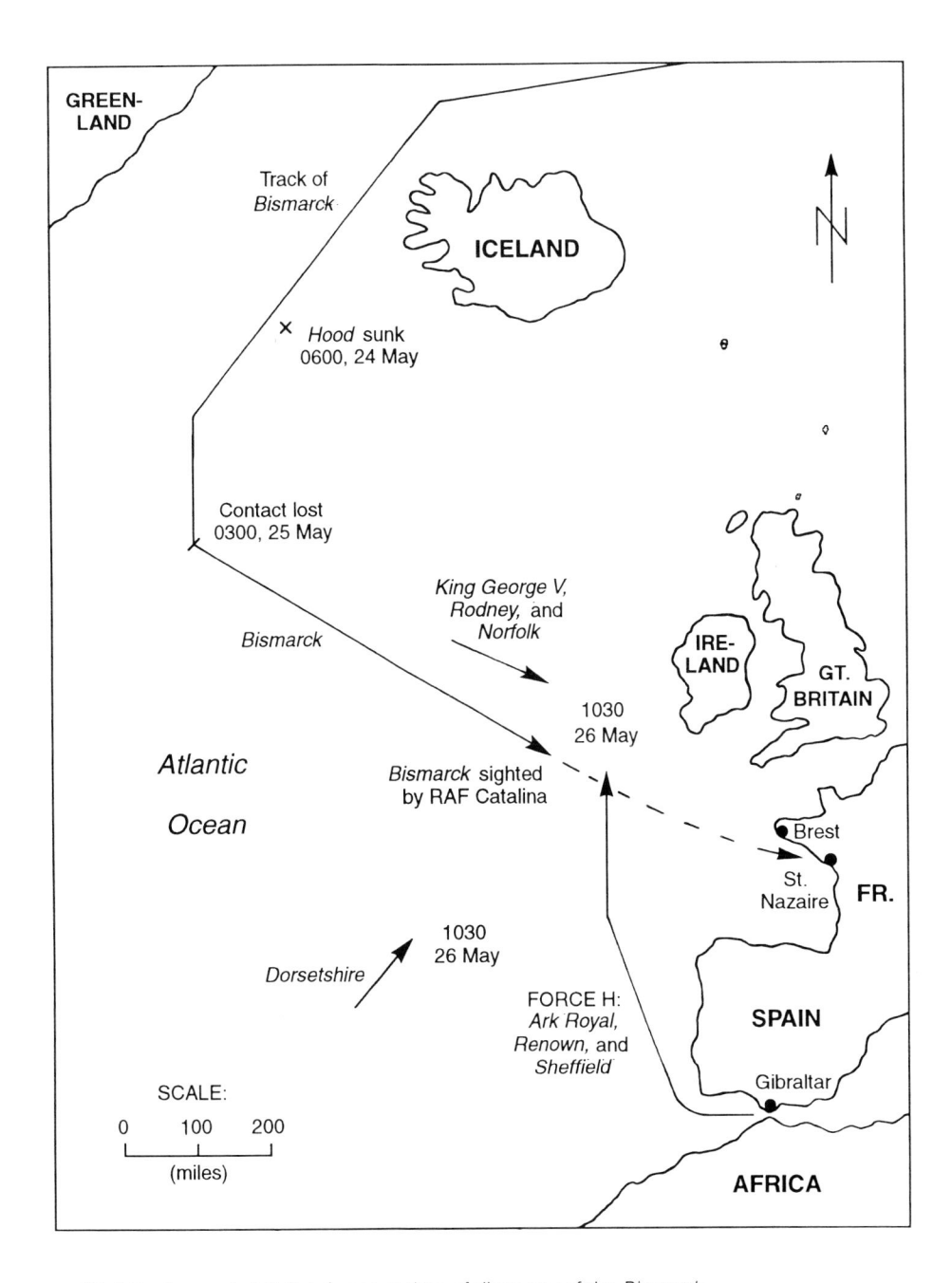

12-1 Deployment of British forces at time of discovery of the *Bismarck*.

That morning Admiral Lütjens, apparently in the belief that he was still under radar observation by the British cruisers that had been trailing him, began transmitting a long message to the German Naval High Command. In this message, he reported on the action that took place on the previous morning against the *Hood* and *Prince of Wales*. He then described the damage sustained by the *Bismarck* and his intention to head for St. Nazaire for necessary repairs. He commented on the effectiveness of British radar and other circumstances that adversely affected the accomplishment of his mission.

The German Naval High Command had not intercepted any further sighting reports from the *Suffolk* since the last one sent out during the night before the *Bismarck* made her attempt to break away. Convinced that contact had actually been broken, they immediately advised Lütjens of this and ordered him to cease transmission. The *Bismarck* had apparently been receiving radar signals from the *Suffolk*, but they were in fact not strong enough to be reflected from the *Bismarck* and be received by the *Suffolk*. Lütjens believed that the British radar had a range in excess of the 25,000 yards it actually had.

The British intercepted Lütjens' transmission at several locations, but their radio direction-finders within range were roughly in a line and therefore could point only in the same general direction. They did not have a direction-finder situated far enough at an angle to the transmission where it could cut across the lines of the other direction-finders and enable them to pin-point its position by triangulation. The direction indicated did, however, give a clue to the course of the *Bismarck* based on the last known position of the ship. It was now almost certain that she was heading for the French coast, and further search efforts would be concentrated in that direction.

After participating in the search for the rest of the day and running low on fuel, the *Prince of Wales* was ordered to return to Iceland. There she unloaded her dead and wounded, took on fuel, and headed for the naval base at Rosyth for repairs. The *Repulse* had also run low on fuel and had to be detached from Tovey's squadron at about noon. This left only the aircraft carrier *Victorious* and several cruisers to assist the *King George V* in the search. By nightfall, ship *Nelson*, was the heaviest in the Royal Navy, being able to throw a broadside of 10 tons of armour-piercing projectiles against a target every 45 seconds. This was one-and-a-half times more than the broadside weights of either the *Hood*, *King George V*-class, or even the *Bismarck*. Two cruisers would also soon be joining Admiral Tovey's force. The *Norfolk* would be returning from Iceland after refuelling, and the heavy cruiser *Dorsetshire*, also a 'County'-class cruiser with eight 8in guns, left her convoy to join in the hunt.

During the afternoon of 25 May, the *Bismarck*'s crew began construction of a dummy funnel that they planned to erect amidships in an attempt to disguise the ship as a British warship. They hoped that it would fool the British, at least from the air, in view of renewed aerial surveillance expected in the morning. With the loss of much of her fuel as a result of the damage inflicted by the *Prince of Wales*, the *Bismarck* was forced to reduce her speed during the day to a more economical 20 knots instead of her maximum sustained speed of 28 knots. A repair crew was later able to bypass some of the damaged pipes and valving and thereby allow part of the fuel reserves earlier cut off to be tapped for use, but this only slightly alleviated the problem.

In the early morning of 26 May, two American-built Consolidated PBY-5 (Catalina) flying boats assigned to RAF Coastal Command took off from their base in Northern Ireland to conduct a

The Bismarck Chase

12–2 RAF Catalina flying-boat sights the *Bismarck* heading for the French coast, 26 May 1941.

long-range search for the *Bismarck*. Shortly after 1000, an observer aboard one of the aircraft spotted the wake of a ship below, and the pilot immediately turned the plane toward the ship for a closer look. As soon as the ship could be identified as a large warship, possibly a battleship, its position was radioed back to their base. The information was relayed to the Admiralty, and with all their ships accounted for, they immediately concluded that the *Bismarck* had been found.

The dummy funnel constructed by the *Bismarck*'s crew had not as yet been erected, but in the end, it would have served no useful purpose. As soon as the Catalina flying boat had come into view, the *Bismarck* immediately opened fire on it with her anti-aircraft batteries, thereby advertising the fact that she was an enemy warship. About an hour after being spotted by the Catalina, the *Bismarck* had another unwelcome intruder, a Swordfish on a scouting mission. By chance, she happened to be in the search pattern of aircraft from the *Ark Royal*, which had just arrived in the area with Force H.

The *Ark Royal* was a one-of-a-kind aircraft carrier laid down in September 1935 at the Cammell Laird Shipyard in Birkenhead. She was launched in April 1937 and completed in November 1938. She displaced 22,000 tons and had a speed of over 30 knots. She had an overall length of 800ft, beam of 95ft, and draught of 28ft. She carried 72 aircraft of different types, twice as many as the *Illustrious*-class could accommodate, but lacked the additional armour protection of that class. Her defensive armament consisted of sixteen 4.5in guns in eight twin turrets, four on each side of the flight deck, and smaller-calibre AA guns.

The *Ark Royal* had participated in numerous operations, including the search for the German pocket battleship *Admiral Graf Spee*, the Norwegian campaign, the attack on French warships at Dakar, and actions against the Italian Navy in the Mediterranean. She was

12–3 The heavy cruiser HMS *Sheffield* of Force H, in 1941. (Imperial War Museum: A6162)

attacked by a U-boat in September 1939, just two weeks after the beginning of the Second World War, and she came under air attack on several occasions in the Mediterranean without being hit.

Soon the light cruiser *Sheffield*, also from Force H, was spotted by the *Bismarck*. She was of the *Southampton*-class completed in 1936. She displaced about 9100 tons and had a speed of 32 knots. She had an overall length of nearly 600ft, beam of 62ft, and draught of 17ft. The *Sheffield* carried twelve 6in guns in four triple turrets, two forward and two aft, six 21in torpedo tubes in two triple mounts amidships on her main deck, one on each side of the ship, and three aircraft. She had a crew of over 700 officers and men.

Now that the *Bismarck* had been discovered, it would just be a matter of time before all of the available resources of the Royal Navy would be thrown against her. Not knowing the disposition of those resources, the Germans were understandably concerned about their chances of survival in view of the seemingly overwhelming odds stacked against them. It would have helped to have had some intelligence from the German Naval High Command about the enemy's movements.

CHAPTER 13

The Bismarck is Disabled

When the Admiralty received the report that the *Bismarck* had been sighted by a flying boat, they immediately plotted her position as well as the location of Royal Navy units in the vicinity. The results of the plot revealed that only Force H was close enough to engage her. At 1030, when the *Bismarck* was located, Force H was in fact ahead of the *Bismarck* and only a short distance north of her course. The battlecruiser *Renown* could have easily closed with the *Bismarck*, but considering her limited firepower and protection, she obviously could not have stopped the battleship by herself. The *King George V* and *Rodney* were too far behind the *Bismarck* to catch her, and there were no other heavy units of the Royal Navy in a position to intercept her on her way to the French coast.

The only hope of destroying the *Bismarck* was to slow her down sufficiently for the battleships to be able to catch up with her. This task obviously fell to the aircraft carrier *Ark Royal*, as only her torpedo planes had the range and weapons to do the job. By the time this plan of action had been decided upon, Force H had already steamed some distance further north before Somerville turned his ships on a course parallel to that of the *Bismarck* at about noon. Force H was still within range, but it would take longer for the aircraft of the *Ark Royal* to reach their target.

Preparations were immediately undertaken to launch an air strike against the *Bismarck* as soon as possible that afternoon. The Swordfish aboard the *Ark Royal* were fuelled, and 18in torpedoes were latched to their underbellies as their crews were being briefed. In mid-afternoon on 26 May, over a dozen aircraft took off from the deck of the *Ark Royal* and headed for the last known position of the *Bismarck*. Their pilots had just been advised that their target was alone in the area, but in fact the light cruiser *Sheffield* had been ordered to move up astern of the *Bismarck* and keep her under observation. The signal concerning the *Sheffield* had not been deciphered on the *Ark Royal* in time to alert the Swordfish pilots.

When this had finally been decoded nearly an hour later, the pilots were warned in the clear to look out for the cruiser. The warning about the *Sheffield* was not received in time, and many of the pilots, having been told earlier that no other ship was in the vicinity, pressed their attack against the first ship they saw. The crew of the *Sheffield* were horrified as they saw their own planes making torpedo runs against their ship, but they held their fire. The cruiser had to take extreme evasive action to avoid the torpedoes aimed at her. By a stroke of luck, several of the torpedoes exploded prematurely as they hit the water, sending up geysers of water directly behind the Swordfish aircraft that had just released them, but sparing the *Sheffield*.

Fortunately, the *Sheffield* was not hit by any of the torpedoes that were launched against her, and a few pilots recognised her in time before they let loose their torpedoes. Some realised that they were attacking the *Sheffield* only after they had dropped their 'fish', but most of the pilots headed back for the *Ark Royal* in a dejected mood

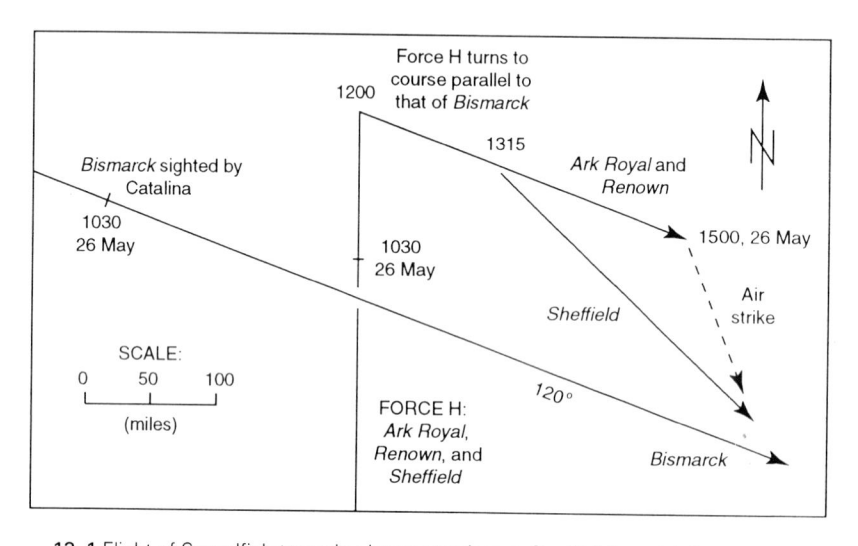

13-1 Flight of Swordfish torpedo planes attack HMS *Sheffield* by mistake.

The Bismarck is Disabled

over their failure to hit the target and the malfunction of many of their torpedoes. When they received the warning, their mood changed to relief as they realised that they could have hit and sunk their own ship and caused many casualties among their naval comrades. All of the planes returned safely about an hour later.

Tovey and the Admiralty were advised that the air strike against the *Bismarck* had been unsuccessful, and hope was beginning to fade that she could be slowed down sufficiently for the battleships to catch up. They realised that it would soon be dark and by the following morning the *Bismarck* would be under friendly air cover making it impossible for the Royal Navy to continue the pursuit. Another air strike, even if one could be launched before nightfall, was not considered to hold too much promise in view of the unsuccessful one just made. The Admiralty and Admiral Tovey were spared the details of that abortive raid against the *Sheffield*.

During the day, morale aboard the *Bismarck* began to drop, from the fleet commander down to the lowest rating, as the interception of radio traffic clearly indicated that units of the Royal Navy were closing on them. Lütjens believed that it was just a matter of time before the *Bismarck* would be surrounded by a far superior force and that the ship would be destroyed. The fuel shortage caused by the *Prince of Wales'* fateful hit required the *Bismarck* to steam at only 20 knots so that she would have sufficient fuel to reach St Nazaire. Topping off her tanks in Norway or from a tanker at sea would certainly have eased the situation, but that had not been done.

The *Bismarck* had a fuel capacity of about 8000 tons, and she would have used about 1000 tons a day at top speed, which would enable her to cover nearly 800 miles a day when travelling at her maximum speed of 28 knots. By the time she arrived at Bergen, she had been down to about 6500 tons (80 per cent of her capacity), and she used another 2000 tons before engaging the *Hood* and *Prince of Wales*. Over 1000 tons of fuel had been contaminated with sea water or made inaccessible due to the hit scored by the *Prince of Wales*. Had the *Bismarck* been able to steam at 28 knots, she would have already been under the protective cover of the Luftwaffe by that afternoon.

As the day wore on and there still had been no attack, hope was beginning to rise on the *Bismarck*. She was still being shadowed by

The Bismarck Chase

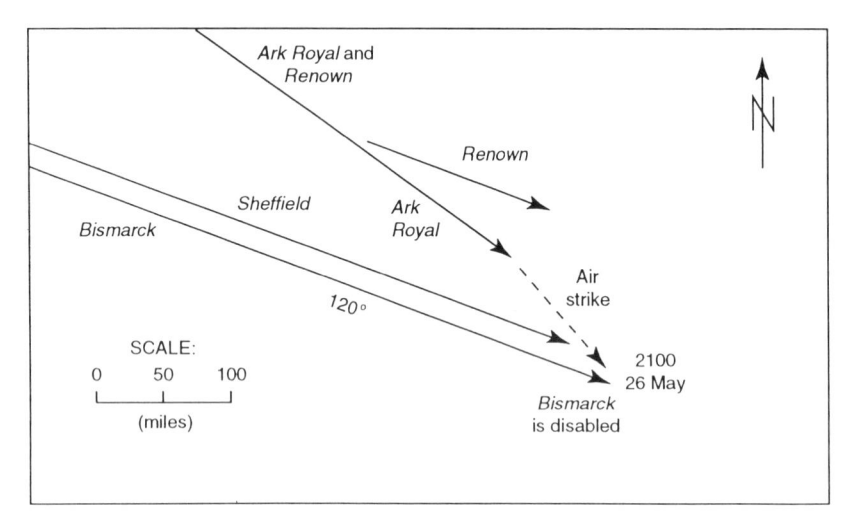

13–2 Second air strike from HMS *Ark Royal* is successful in disabling the *Bismarck*.

the *Sheffield*, but the crew was surprised that they had not been attacked. They knew that an aircraft carrier was in the area from the earlier sighting of a Swordfish. Of course, they were unaware of the abortive raid conducted in mid-afternoon against the *Sheffield*, so they had every reason to hope of escape as night approached. In another couple of hours, they would come under the concealing mantle of darkness, and by morning, they would be 'out of the woods' completely and under the protective wings of the Luftwaffe.

Aboard the *Ark Royal*, feverish attempts were being made to get the aircraft turned around for another strike. There would be enough light for just one more attempt, and it was vital that it be made before the *Bismarck* got home 'Scot-free'. The torpedoes used on the earlier strike had been fitted with a new type of magnetic detonator that was intended to go off beneath the target when activated by the magnetic influence of a ship's hull. While good in theory, they were prone to explode from the shock of the torpedo hitting the water. Not wanting a repeat of the previous fiasco, mechanics replaced them with conventional contact detonators on the torpedoes now being loaded on the Swordfish.

Once the planes were ready and their pilots given a final briefing, the Swordfish took off again and headed for the *Bismarck*. This time

The Bismarck is Disabled

13–7 Captain Philip Vian, commanding the 4th Destroyer Flotilla. (Imperial War Museum: A1595)

Returning to Germany with 300 prisoners taken from the ships sunk by the pocket battleship, the *Altmark* was intercepted by British warships off the southern coast of Norway near Stavanger. She turned into a small fjord for protection, but the *Cossack* followed her in. When the *Altmark* became grounded in the fjord, crewmen from the *Cossack* boarded her and forcibly freed the prisoners who were then returned to England.

At first, Vian's destroyers merely shadowed the *Bismarck*, but then they set up a cordon around her with two destroyers on each flank, one ahead and one astern, and the *Cossack* bringing up the rear. Shortly after dark, Vian ordered his destroyers to make a synchronised torpedo attack against the *Bismarck*. As his ships fanned out to execute the attack from different directions, they came under intense and accurate fire. They launched their torpedoes from a couple of miles away, and even though they believed that several hits were scored, there was no apparent impact on the *Bismarck*.

During the night, the destroyers made several individual attacks with gunfire as well as torpedoes, but again to no apparent effect. After that, Vian kept his destroyers in contact with the *Bismarck*, but at a safer distance out of range of her main armament. As dawn approached, the *Piorun* had to be detached to refuel, and the remaining destroyers resumed their box formation to keep the *Bismarck* under surveillance from all quarters.

As night fell, all aboard the *Bismarck* finally realised that their situation was hopeless. The fickle Gods of War appeared to have turned their favour toward the British after blessing the Germans for the last couple of days. They were still some 500 miles away from Brest, the closest point on the French coast, and well beyond the range of Luftwaffe support. They were told by the German Naval High Command that U-boats were on their way to help them, but they knew that there was little that any U-boats could do to save the *Bismarck*. All they could do was wait for the end which they fully expected would come in the morning, and they were under no illusions that they would be as lucky as they were when they met the *Hood* and *Prince of Wales*.

The officers and professional seamen probably accepted their fate in the tradition of the *Kriegsmarine*, as did the idealistic young cadets. Those who had families or had been conscripted into the service may have had other hopes than dying for the Fatherland and Third Reich. Some may have remembered that their comrades

The Bismarck is Disabled

aboard the *Admiral Graf Spee* were spared that fate when the decision was made to scuttle their ship rather than face overwhelming odds, but that of course was a completely different situation. The *Bismarck* was still capable of putting up a fight and inflicting some damage to the enemy, so it would come down to everyone doing their duty regardless of the consequences.

The correspondents aboard the *Bismarck* were non-combatants, but they knew that incoming fire would not be able to distinguish between themselves and legitimate targets of war. They had plenty to write about, but had no way to file their reports. They undoubtedly interviewed many crew members of the *Bismarck* and had woven heroic tales of their exploits in the battle in the Denmark Strait, but they probably now realised that it would all be for nothing. They were prepared to cover the forthcoming battle that was expected in the morning, but their own self-preservation became uppermost in some minds.

During the night, there was an exchange of messages between the *Bismarck* and the German Naval High Command. Lütjens advised his superiors of the air strike, the fatal torpedo hit, and the inability of his ship to manoeuvre. In reporting the hopelessness of the situation, he added that he would fight to the last shell and ended with a greeting to the Führer. German Naval Group West advised him of the dispatch of tugs to the scene and plans for Luftwaffe coverage in the morning, but Lütjens did not really expect that such support would materialise in time to save his ship.

The messages continued through the early morning hours. The German Naval High Command and Group West sent their best wishes and even Hitler thanked the Fleet Commander in the name of the entire German nation for his devotion to duty. The Führer also addressed a message to the crew of the *Bismarck*, promising that everything possible would be done to save them and commending them for their performance of duty. Based on the recommendation of Lütjens, Adalbert Schneider, Chief Gunnery Officer of the *Bismarck*, was awarded the Knight's Cross for sinking the *Hood*.

Lütjens and the German Naval High Command were anxious to save the *Bismarck*'s War Diary, which would explain in detail

13–8 The erratic wake left by the *Bismarck* after she was crippled by the Swordfish's torpedo. (Imperial War Museum: C2456)

The Bismarck is Disabled

everything that occurred during the sortie and therefore might be of help in planning future operations with surface ships. Lütjens ordered the War Diary to be flown out by one of the Arado 196 float planes carried aboard, but the catapult had been damaged making it useless. The aircraft, loaded with fuel, was jettisoned overboard to avoid it becoming a fire hazard during the battle. He then requested that a U-boat be sent to retrieve the Diary, and although this was promised by German Naval Group West, no submarine reached the *Bismarck* in time to save it.

CHAPTER 14

The Final Battle

Morale was high aboard the British ships, and their crews knew that they would soon have the opportunity to avenge their comrades who went down with the *Hood* and those who were killed and injured on the *Prince of Wales*. The *Bismarck* was still a dangerous adversary, but there was no longer any question about the outcome of the forthcoming battle. Since the German ship was apparently going nowhere, the British could dictate the time and circumstances of their attack. With the *King George V* and *Rodney* being able to approach the *Bismarck* from different directions and divide her fire, it would be almost like a 'turkey shoot'. It would certainly be a far cry from the situation that the *Hood* and *Prince of Wales* had had to face a couple of days earlier.

As dawn broke on the morning of 27 May, Admiral Tovey manoeuvred his squadron so that it would approach the *Bismarck* from the west and have the target silhouetted by the morning light. The *King George V* and *Rodney* sailed in line abreast about 600 yards apart toward the last reported position of the enemy. The *Bismarck*, still moving slowly on a meandering course, finally came into view to the south-east at about 0850 and at a range of about 22,000 yards (12–13 miles). As soon as the enemy was sighted, the *Rodney* peeled off to port and headed on a more easterly course to engage the *Bismarck* separately as prearranged.

Tovey did not want his ships to be too close together so that a salvo from the *Bismarck* that missed one ship would have a chance of hitting the other. With the *King George V* and *Rodney* initially only 600 yards apart, it would have been possible for the *Bismarck* to fire between them and have a good chance of hitting either of them if her aim were just a little off. It might have even been possible for the *Bismarck* to hit both ships with the same salvo if the spread of

The Final Battle

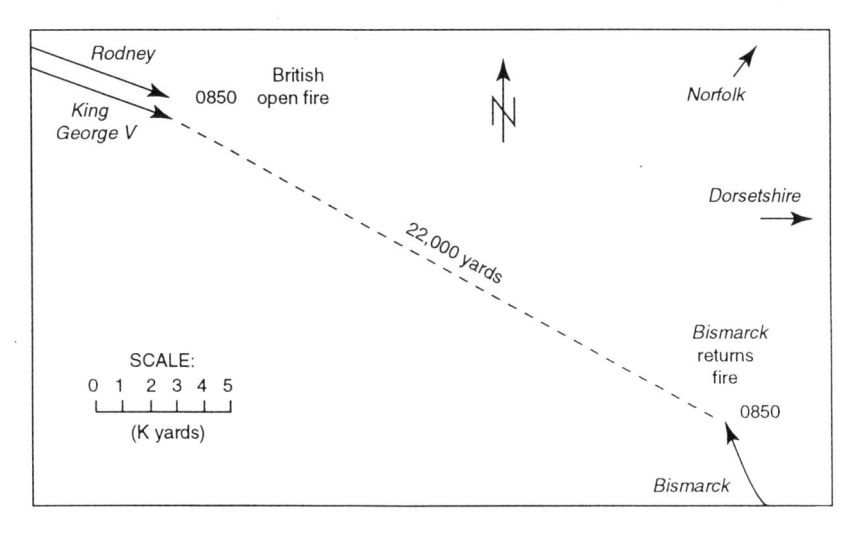

14-1 Position of British and German forces when the British opened fire (0850).

shot was wide enough. By this manoeuvre, however, each ship became a separate target, and the *Bismarck* would have to split her fire to engage both of them.

The *Rodney* quickly determined the range and course of the *Bismarck*. The guns of her two foremost turrets were raised to an elevation of 13° as those turrets were traversed to the azimuth corresponding to the bearing of the target. With her third turret unable to bear due to the acute angle of approach, she opened fire with only two turrets. A minute later, the *King George V* followed suit with a salvo from both of her forward turrets. As with the *Rodney*, the rear turret of the *King George V* could not be traversed forward enough to be aimed at the *Bismarck*. Both ships continued on their respective courses for another 10 minutes, firing all the while with their forward guns.

Throughout the early morning, spotters on the *Bismarck* maintained a sharp vigil for any new threat that might develop. They could occasionally see Vian's destroyers in the distance as they were keeping up their surveillance, but they were more interested in any heavy units of the Royal Navy that might be in the vicinity. At first light, all of the rangefinders and telescopes swept the horizon for any signs of other British warships which they expected

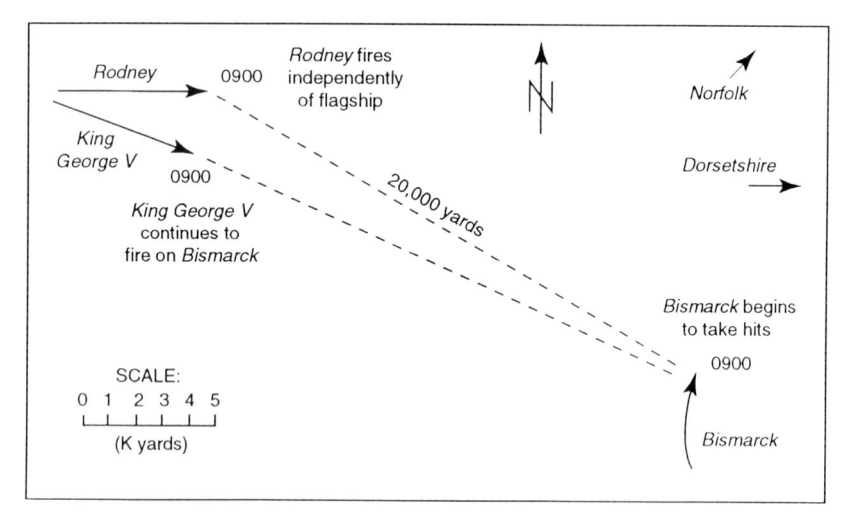

14–2 HMS *King George V* and *Rodney* separate to split the *Bismarck*'s return fire.

would soon be on the scene. They were not disappointed as the faint outlines of the *King George V* and *Rodney*, approaching from the north-east, came into their sights.

Although wallowing in the heavy swells with little stability, the *Bismarck* took up the challenge. By using her port engine, she was able to turn slowly to starboard and bring all of her turrets to bear on the oncoming enemy. Her gunners were able to easily identify one of the ships as being of the *Nelson*-class due to her extraordinarily long foredeck mounting all three main turrets. The other ship looked strikingly similar to the *King George V*, which the Germans mistakenly believed to have been the *Hood*'s companion instead of the *Prince of Wales*. They probably reasoned that the *King George V* had really not been damaged as seriously as they first believed and was therefore able to return to battle.

Realising that the *Nelson*-class ship, with her nine 16in guns, was the greater threat, Lütjens ordered that she be the initial target. When her rangefinders had the range to the target, the *Bismarck* opened fire with several salvoes against the *Rodney*. Her gunnery was good as ever, and she soon straddled the *Rodney*, sending shell splinters slicing through the air and onto the ship. Not wanting to leave her other opponent unengaged, she then trained her guns on

The Final Battle

the *King George V* and fired a couple of well-placed salvoes in that direction. The onset of action gave many members of the German crew something to do and must have helped take their minds off what they believed to be their impending doom.

By 0900, the range was down to 20,000 yards, and both the *King George V* and *Rodney*, firing constantly with only their forward turrets, were beginning to score hits. At that time, Tovey ordered both ships to turn to starboard so that they could fire with their full broadsides. This placed both ships on a course that was almost due south with the *King George V* in the lead and the *Rodney* only a short distance to the rear and a little closer to the *Bismarck*. At that time, the *Bismarck* was moving northward toward the British ships. They maintained that course for another 10–15 minutes, and by that time the *Bismarck* was almost directly off the port beam of the *King George V*.

As the *Bismarck* continued to move across the line of fire from the British ships, Captain Dalrymple-Hamilton turned the *Rodney* around at about 0915 to keep from blocking the flagship's field of fire. Soon the *King George V* also turned so that she could keep up with the *Bismarck*. Both ships, now firing to starboard, kept up a continuous cannonade against their target. By 0920, the range had come down to 15,000 yards (9 miles) for the *King George V* and 10,000 yards (6 miles) for the *Rodney*. They continued to blast away with all of their heavy guns, scoring hit after hit as the range slowly closed. By then, the *Norfolk* and *Dorsetshire* had also entered the fray and began firing with their eight 8in guns.

While the *Bismarck* was able to put up some resistance at first, she slowly succumbed to the overwhelming weight of firepower directed against her. One by one, her guns fell silent as direct hits were scored on her turrets and fire control directors, and by 0930 all of her main guns were put out of action. With little forward motion, she just rolled in the swells, making it difficult to direct her gunfire. She was able to cause only some minor damage to the *Rodney* with near-misses before her main armament was disabled. Her secondary armament of twelve 5.9in guns played little part in this or the previous engagement against the *Hood* and *Prince of Wales*.

Wanting still more hits, Tovey ordered both battleships to close even further. By 0940, the range was down to 4000 yards (2 miles),

The Bismarck Chase

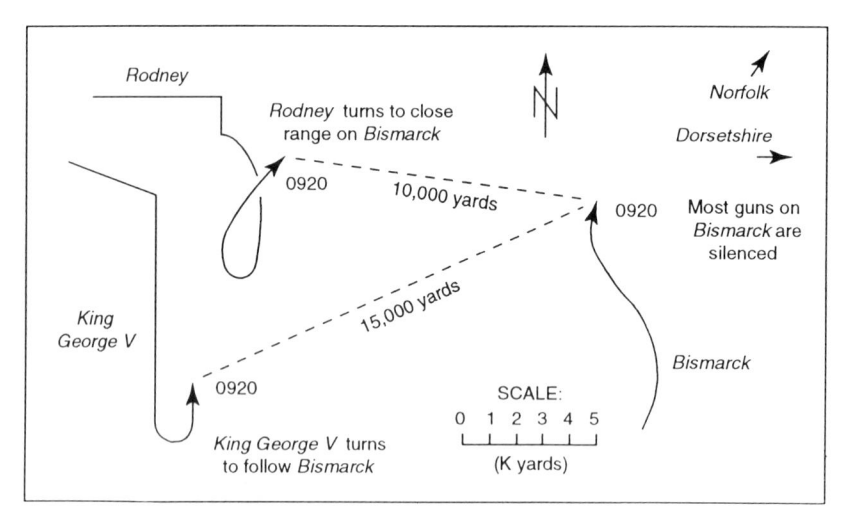

14-3 HMS *King George V* and *Rodney* manoeuvre to keep their guns trained on *Bismarck*.

and the *Rodney* was firing point-blank into the hulk of the *Bismarck*. The *Norfolk* and *Dorsetshire* also closed in, while the *King George V* continued to pound the enemy from a range of 12,000 yards. Tovey was anxious to settle the issue as soon as possible so that his ships could disengage before their fuel situation became critical. At 1000, the *Bismarck* was still flying her ensign and showing no signs of capitulating even after the tremendous punishment she received during the hour or more since the British ships first opened fire.

The *Bismarck*'s superstructure had been reduced to a shambles from direct hits and near-misses. Her forward tower mast and funnel were riddled with armour-piercing shell and fragments leaving a wide variety of jagged holes. Lightly-armoured portions of her hull and decks were penetrated by numerous projectiles which exploded with devastating effect inside the ship. Many fires were started within the ship, but under the circumstances, little could be done to contain them. Hundreds of her crew members were killed and wounded at their battle stations by the hail of steel and explosives that was rained down on the ship.

With the *Bismarck* now a completely helpless wreck and unable to inflict any more damage on the enemy, the order was given to open the valves to the sea and to set scuttling charges to sink the ship.

The Final Battle

14-4 HMS *Rodney* after her 180° turn to keep clear of HMS *King George V*'s field of fire. (Imperial War Museum: MH15931)

The torpedo and underwater shell hits already received were not sufficient to ensure that the *Bismarck* would go under promptly. Once the charges had been set, the order was given to abandon ship. It was every man for himself as those below deck came up to face the murderous fire still falling on the stricken vessel. One by one, the crew members of the *Bismarck* who had survived the ordeal so far jumped off the ship.

The Bismarck Chase

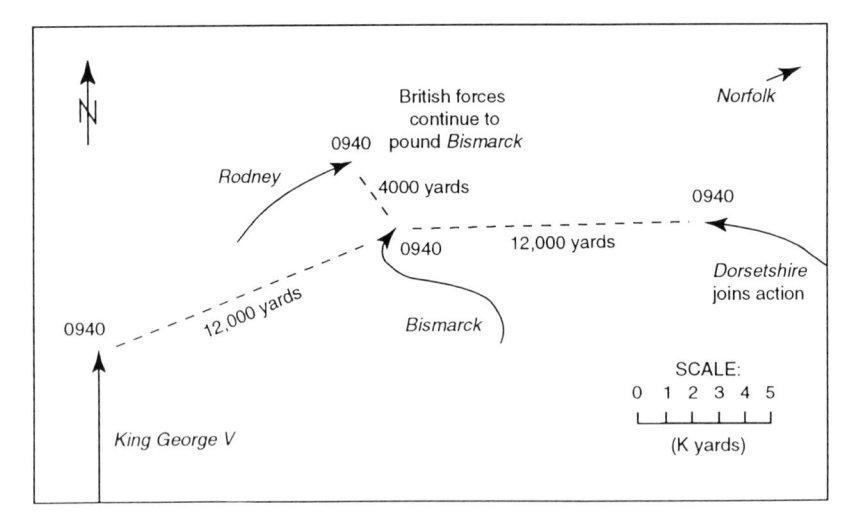

14–5 HMS *Rodney* closes the range while HMS *Dorsetshire* joins the action.

14–6 *Bismarck* continues to be pounded by the British ships. (Imperial War Museum: MISC 50789)

The Final Battle

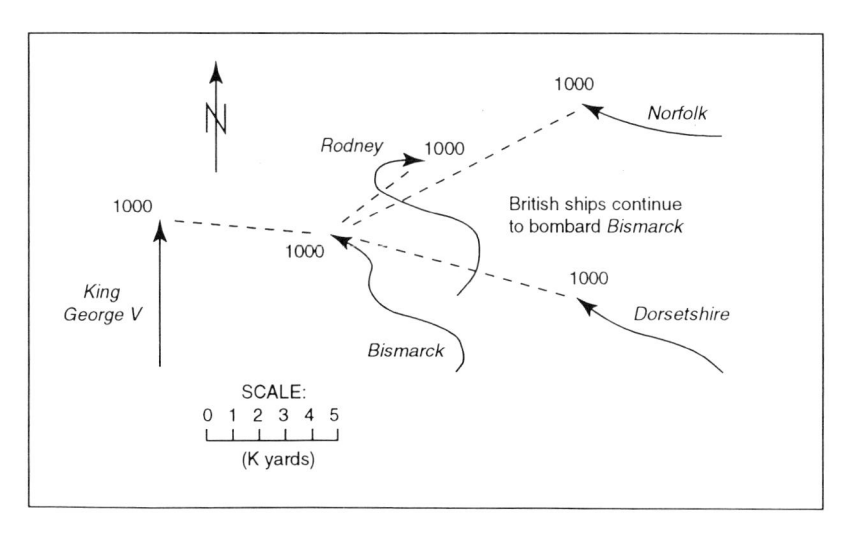

14–7 HMS *Norfolk* adds her firepower to the bombardment of the *Bismarck*.

With the *Bismarck* still defiantly flying her ensign, the British had no alternative but to continue to fire on the ship until the Germans capitulated or the *Bismarck* was sunk. Both British battleships were running critically low on fuel and would soon have to break off the action. Seeing that gunnery would not be able to deliver the knockout blow that would send the *Bismarck* to the bottom, Tovey ordered the battleships to cease fire and return to base. The destroyers *Mashona* and *Tartar* had already turned back due to their being low on fuel. Captain Vian's destroyers were not only low on fuel but also out of torpedoes, so there was no point in their remaining. The *Norfolk* had just fired its last remaining torpedoes at the *Bismarck* and turned to depart, leaving only the *Dorsetshire* on the scene with any torpedoes.

The *Dorsetshire* was therefore ordered to finish off the *Bismarck*. The cruiser steamed into position off the *Bismarck*'s starboard beam and fired two torpedoes that hit amidships. She then steamed around her quarry and scored an additional hit on her port side. While these hits in themselves may not have been mortal, there is little question that they added to the underwater damage sustained by the *Bismarck* and contributed to her ultimate demise.

The *Bismarck* was dead in the water and slowly sinking. The firing was over, and the remaining survivors were able to leave the

The Bismarck Chase

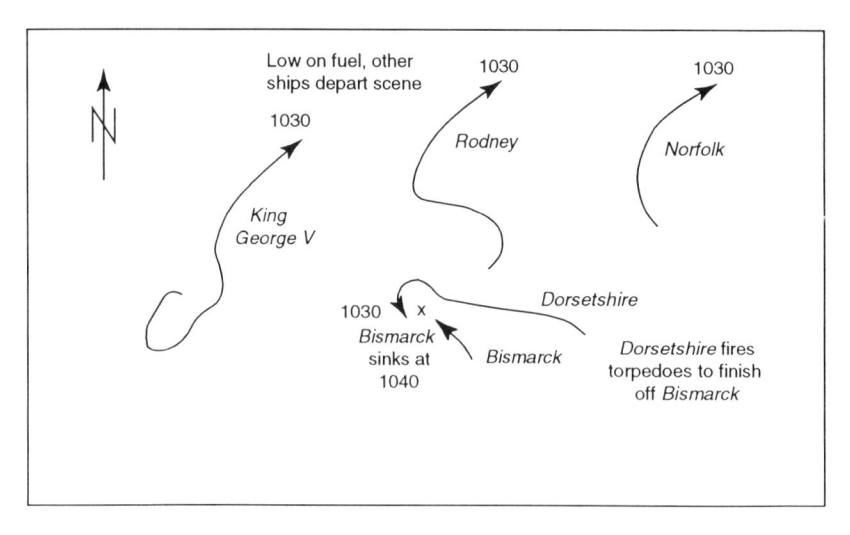

14–8 HMS *Dorsetshire* fires her last torpedoes at *Bismarck* while other Royal Navy units depart.

ship in relative safety. By then, there were hundreds of men in the water, which was cold but not as icy as the survivors of the *Hood* had had to face. All they could do was watch their ship go down and hope for rescue by British ships. The *Bismarck* continued to settle by the stern and take on a list to port. As her list increased, she finally turned turtle and continued to go down stern-first. Some of her crew members, not being able to jump off the *Bismarck* as she was turning over, scrambled over the side onto the bottom of the hull and left the ship from there.

As the *Bismarck* turned on her side, her damaged forward tower mast, funnel, and rear mainmast were beginning to break away at their bases. The weight of those unsupported structures were pulling them over and causing them to fall downward. When they hit the water, the protruding structures were then forced upward and completely torn away from their moorings. The ship continued to roll over, and those structures, as well as any other loose equipment and debris on her decks, fell into the sea and sank. Her heavy anchors stowed at the edge of the deck on both sides of the ship broke away from their hold-down fittings and also plunged into the deep.

When she had turned completely upside-down, her four main gun turrets, weighing nearly 1900 tons apiece, slid out of their

The Final Battle

14-9 The last photograph of the *Bismarck*, taken from HMS *Dorsetshire*. (Imperial War Museum: A4386)

barbettes and sank to the bottom of the ocean. The turrets were merely resting on the bearings mounted on the barbettes and were held in place by gravity alone. The ring gear (a large ring with internal teeth corresponding in size of the barbette) attached to the underside of each turret, which allowed the turret to be rotated in its barbette by a motor-driven spur gear, did not impede their fall. The *Bismarck*'s bow slipped below the waves at about 1040,

The Bismarck Chase

14-10 Survivors from the *Bismarck* picked up by HMS *Dorsetshire*. (Imperial War Museum: ZZZ 3130C)

bringing to an end a short but highly eventful career, marked by initial victory and then ultimate defeat.

The *Dorsetshire* was ordered to pick up survivors, so the cruiser slowly sailed into the mass of humanity in the water where the *Bismarck* went down. Ropes were thrown over the side for the survivors to climb up, with the assistance of the British seamen. The

The Final Battle

Dorsetshire had taken on board nearly 80 German sailors, and the destroyer *Maori* had picked up about 25 more when suddenly there was a submarine alert. The *Dorsetshire* immediately got underway, leaving hundreds of survivors behind, some still clinging to the ropes along her side before they dropped off. Captain Martin knew that U-boats were on their way to the scene and did not want his ship to be a sitting duck for them. The *Maori* wisely followed suit and also left the area.

The abrupt departure of the British ships sounded the death knell for nearly all of the several hundred survivors left behind in the water, but the British commanders had no other choice. If a U-boat had come upon the scene, there is no question that its captain would have attacked at the British ships, even with the knowledge that there may have been *Bismarck* survivors on board. Difficult as it was, the decision to leave the area was the only possible course of action that could have been taken under the circumstances.

The Admiralty was immediately notified of the *Bismarck*'s sinking, and the information was passed directly to the Prime Minister. Churchill was addressing Parliament at the time, and he interrupted his speech to announce the welcome news that the *Bismarck* had been sunk. All were relieved that the threat had been eliminated, and there was great satisfaction that the *Hood* had been avenged. The episode had been far too costly for any wild celebration, and the loss of the *Hood* still weighed heavily on the minds of all.

When the British announced that they had sunk the *Bismarck*, the German Naval High Command tried to reach Admiral Lütjens, but received no reply. With no word from the ship for several hours, they had to assume the worst. Hitler was notified, but not being deeply interested in naval matters, he merely expressed disappointment that his navy had let him down and left him with a propaganda defeat. He was preoccupied with the ongoing airborne assault on the island of Crete and plans for the forthcoming invasion of the Soviet Union only weeks away.

The toll of human life and equipment for this episode did not end with the sinking of the *Bismarck*. On the morning of 28 May, the Germans sent a fleet of bombers to attack the Home Fleet on its way back to Scapa Flow, but they found only the destroyers *Mashona*

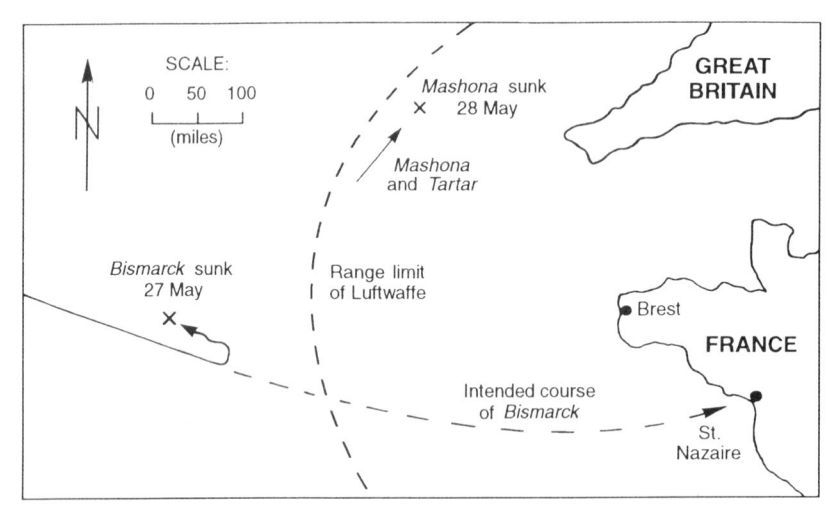

14-11 Position of *Bismarck* relative to the French coast at time of sinking.

and *Tartar* of the Sixth Destroyer Flotilla heading for Londonderry at low speed to conserve fuel. They attacked the hapless destroyers and succeeded in hitting the *Mashona*, which sank with the loss of nearly 50 officers and men. The *Tartar* was able to rescue 170 men, including *Mashona*'s skipper, and bring them to Londonderry with her fuel nearly exhausted.

On the morning following the sinking of the *Bismarck*, five more survivors were rescued by the German weather ship *Sachsenwald* and by one of the U-boats that had been sent to the scene. Other U-boats scoured the area, but could find only floating debris and patches of oil. Out of her total complement of 2200 men, there were less than 110 survivors. On 30 May, the *Dorsetshire* dropped off her cargo of *Bismarck* survivors at Newcastle and the *Maori* landed hers at a base on the Clyde. From there, the survivors went to London for interrogation, and they were then sent to sit out the war in prisoner of war camps.

Thus ended Operation 'Rhine Exercise'. While the *Bismarck* and the *Prinz Eugen* initially scored a major tactical victory over the *Hood* and the *Prince of Wales*, in the end they suffered a strategic defeat of even greater proportions. Although the *Hood* was sunk and the *Prince of Wales* was forced to disengage, that task force was successful in inflicting sufficient damage on the *Bismarck* to cause

The Final Battle

her to abort her mission and head to France for repairs. This enabled other British forces to eventually hunt down the German flagship and sink it. Britain not only thwarted the German attempt to break out into the North Atlantic to attack Allied shipping, but she had also destroyed their only operational battleship.

In chess terms, it was like sacrificing a pawn to take one of your opponent's knights or rooks. The British still had fifteen capital ships after the loss of the *Hood* and the battleship *Royal Oak*, which was torpedoed by a U-boat while anchored at Scapa Flow early in the war. Soon she would have three additional battleships of the *King George V*-class which were currently under construction – the *Duke of York*, *Anson*, and *Howe*. On the other hand, the Germans were down to only three capital ships, and even those were no immediate threat. The battleship *Tirpitz* was not yet ready for operational deployment, and the *Gneisenau* and *Scharnhorst* were both undergoing repairs at Brest.

Although Britain suffered a grievous loss in the sinking of the *Hood*, the pride of the Royal Navy, she did not suffer as many casualties as the Germans in this confrontation – 1500 as against 2200. Even the survivors of the *Bismarck* were lost to the Germans as they spent the rest of the war in British prisoner-of-war camps. In contrast, most of the British wounded in the engagement were able to return to service. The total death toll of Operation 'Rhine Exercise' amounted to over 3560 officers and men on both sides.

While conflicting claims were made as to what caused the sinking the *Bismarck* (gunfire, torpedoes, or her own scuttling charges), undoubtedly all of those contributed to her final demise. The scuttling charges certainly accelerated her sinking, but the cumulative effect of all of the shells and torpedoes that had struck her below the waterline probably resulted in sufficient damage that would have caused her to gradually sink anyway. In any event, the argument is purely academic since the *Bismarck* was sunk directly or indirectly as a result of British action, and her threat to Allied shipping was foiled.

CHAPTER 15

Epilogue

After the *Prinz Eugen* was detached from the *Bismarck* in the evening of 24 May, she continued steaming south towards the convoy routes. Two days later, she rendezvoused with the German tanker *Spichern* to take on fuel. She cruised for the next couple of days looking for merchant ships, but did not run across any. On 29 May, she developed engine trouble and had to abort her mission. She arrived at Brest on 1 June to undergo repairs and await further orders, possibly to team up with the battlecruisers *Gneisenau* and *Scharnhorst* also at Brest. Early in July 1941, she was damaged in an air raid and required further repairs.

Giving up on the use of French bases for surface-ship operations due to the vulnerability of their ships to air attacks, the German Naval High Command ordered the *Prinz Eugen*, together with the *Gneisenau* and *Scharnhorst*, to return to Germany. In February 1942, the three ships made their famous 'Channel Dash' right up the English Channel under an umbrella of German fighter cover to reach their bases. Although attacked by British bombers and torpedo planes, the ships succeeded in their attempt, but both the *Gneisenau* and *Scharnhorst* were damaged by mines.

A few days after the Channel Dash, the *Prinz Eugen* was off the coast of Norway when she was hit by a torpedo from the British submarine *Trident*. The explosion nearly tore off her stern, and she had to be fitted with a temporary stern before returning to Germany for repairs. In October 1944, she accidentally rammed the light cruiser *Leipzig* during manoeuvres in the Baltic Sea, and had to be fitted with a new bow. The *Prinz Eugen* remained in the Baltic waters for the rest of the war, providing support to the German ground forces retreating from the east.

Epilogue

15–1 *Prinz Eugen* after her surrender to the Royal Navy at Copenhagen, with HMS *Devonshire* in the background, 26 May 1945. (Imperial War Museum: HU1000)

The 'lucky' *Prinz Eugen* survived the war and was surrendered to the British at Copenhagen in May 1945. She was subsequently taken to Wilhelmshaven where she was turned over to the US Navy. In January 1946, she sailed with a joint German-American crew to Boston, and she then sailed with an all-American crew through the Panama Canal into the Pacific. There she became one of the target ships during the atomic bomb tests at Bikini Atoll in the summer of that year. She survived that test and was towed to Kwajalein Atoll where she sank unexpectedly in December 1946, probably as the result of latent underwater damage sustained in the test.

After the damage inflicted by the *Bismarck* and *Prinz Eugen* had been repaired, the *Prince of Wales* returned to service. In August 1941, she carried Winston Churchill and his staff to Newfoundland for his famous meeting with President Roosevelt which culminated in the Atlantic Charter, and was then sent to the Mediterranean for convoy duty. In October of that year, the *Prince of Wales*, still under the command of Captain Leach, was ordered to sail for Singapore with the destroyers *Electra* and *Express* as Force Z under the overall command of Admiral Sir Thomas Phillips. Their objective was to deter any Japanese aggression against British interests in the area in view of their growing threat to south-east Asia.

The battlecruiser *Repulse*, which had been on convoy duty in the Indian Ocean, was ordered to join Force Z at Ceylon, and from there, the ships sailed for Singapore. They arrived on 2 December 1941, where they were joined by two additional destroyers, the *Encounter* and *Jupiter*. Force Z was also assigned an aircraft carrier, but with the grounding of the new carrier *Indomitable* off Jamaica and the sinking of the *Ark Royal* by a U-boat near Gibraltar, no other carrier could be spared. The situation had become ominous with the sighting by an RAF reconnaissance plane of a large Japanese convoy with a heavy naval escort heading south along the coast of Indo-China on 4 December. Two days later, it was approaching British Malaya.

On 8 December, the British naval commanders met at Singapore to assess the Japanese threat and to plan appropriate countermeasures. They had just received news of the attack on Pearl Harbor a few hours earlier (7 December in Hawaii), and they now anticipated an attack against Malaya. Shortly before nightfall, Force Z set sail in a northerly direction to intercept the reported Japanese convoy. The destroyers *Encounter* and *Jupiter*, both of which needed repairs, had been replaced by two older ships, the *Tenedos* and the Australian *Vampire*. The next day, the Japanese launched an air attack against targets in Malaya, which caused the evacuation of the only airfield that could provide air cover for Admiral Phillips' squadron.

On 9 December, Force Z had been spotted by a Japanese submarine and later by naval aircraft launched from Japanese cruisers. The Japanese attempted to mount an air attack on Force Z that night, but in the darkness, they could not find the British ships. In the meanwhile, the destroyer *Tenedos* was running low on fuel and had to return to Singapore, leaving Phillips with only three destroyers to cover his force. On the morning of 10 December, Admiral Phillips received a report that the Japanese were making a landing at Kuantan, much further down the Malay coast and closer

Epilogue

to Singapore. Sensing this to be an even greater threat, he turned his squadron around and headed south-west toward the reported landing site.

At about 1000 on 10 December, the Japanese discovered the *Tenedos* on her way back to Singapore and subjected her to high-level bombing attacks, but without success. The *Repulse* launched her Walrus seaplane to make a reconnaissance flight in the area of the reported landing at Kuantan, but the pilot could see nothing unusual – the earlier report had evidently been false. Admiral Phillips soon learned of the air attack on the *Tenedos*, and shortly before 1100, a Japanese aircraft was sighted in the distance. He ordered his ships to be brought up to full alert and to increase speed in anticipation of an air attack against the force. He did not have to wait long before a large flight of enemy aircraft was spotted on radar.

At about 1115, the first squadron of Japanese bombers appeared on the scene and attacked the *Repulse*. They scored one hit and several near misses and caused some moderate damage to the ship. Some 15 minutes later, the *Prince of Wales* became the target of a combined bombing and torpedo attack, and was hit by two torpedoes on her port side. One of the torpedoes struck in the stern, damaging her rudder and drive shafts, and the other torpedo hit amidships, causing some flooding. The two torpedo hits left the *Prince of Wales* in a crippled condition and listing to port.

At about noon, the *Repulse* was again attacked and hit by several torpedoes. These hits inflicted fatal wounds on the old battlecruiser, and a half an hour later, she sank. The destroyers *Express* and *Vampire* were ordered to pick up survivors. They managed to rescue nearly 800 men, including Captain Tennant, from the *Repulse*'s complement of about 1310 officers and men. Over 510 officers and men went down with the ship.

The Japanese then turned their full attention to the *Prince of Wales*, which received two more torpedo hits and several near misses by bombs that caused further underwater damage to the ship. This additional damage left her in a sinking condition, and the order was given to abandon ship. The destroyer *Electra* came alongside to take off her crew, but the *Prince of Wales* capsized and sank before that operation could be completed. In all, nearly 1300 officers

The Bismarck Chase

15–2 HMS *Prince of Wales* leaving Singapore on 8 December 1941. She was sunk by Japanese aircraft 2 days later. (Imperial War Museum: A29068)

and men were rescued out of a total complement of over 1600. Among the 325 officers and men that perished with the *Prince of Wales* were Admiral Phillips and Captain Leach.

The battleship *Rodney*, although not hit by the *Bismarck* during the final engagement, nevertheless suffered severe structural damage as a result of stresses imposed by firing full broadsides with her nine 16in guns. She had to undergo major repairs in an American shipyard and was laid up for several months before she

Epilogue

could rejoin the fleet. She survived the war and was finally scrapped in 1948. The battleship *King George V* was kept in service until 1957 before she was scrapped. The carrier *Victorious* was rebuilt in 1950 and again in 1958, but she was also scrapped in 1969 after 28 years of service with the Royal Navy.

After the operation against the *Bismarck*, the *Ark Royal* returned with Force H to Gibraltar. While on convoy duty in the Mediterranean, she was attacked many times by German bombers hoping to avenge the *Bismarck*, but she survived all of these attacks without damage. But on 13 November 1941, the *Ark Royal* was hit by a single

15–3 HMS *Ark Royal* sinking after being torpedoed on 13 December 1941. (Imperial War Museum: A6334)

torpedo from a U-boat near Gibraltar, but that hit proved to be fatal. Nearly all of her crew were rescued by her destroyer escort as she slowly settled on her starboard side. On the following morning, the *Ark Royal*, one of the most renowned ships of the Royal Navy, turned over and sank.

The heavy cruiser *Dorsetshire*, which struck the last blow against the *Bismarck* with her three torpedoes, was also sent the Far East to bolster the British fleet operating in the Indian Ocean. On 5 April 1942 (Easter Sunday), the *Dorsetshire* and her sister ship, the *Cornwall*, came under attack by Japanese dive-bombers off Ceylon. Both ships received multiple bomb hits and sank with heavy loss of life. The *Suffolk* and *Norfolk* both survived the war and were eventually scrapped in 1948 and 1950 respectively. The *Sheffield* also survived the war and was scrapped in 1967.

The destroyer *Electra*, which had rescued the three survivors from the *Hood* and later had taken hundreds of officers and men from the sinking *Prince of Wales*, returned to Singapore. When the Japanese army came down the Malay Peninsula and approached Singapore, the *Electra* was dispatched to reinforce the Allied Western Striking Force defending the Dutch East Indies from Japanese invasion. On 27 February 1942, she was one of the Allied warships sunk by a superior Japanese force during the Battle of the Java Sea. Of her crew of nearly 150 officers and men, over 90 were lost.

The destroyer *Cossack* was torpedoed in the North Atlantic later in 1941 and sank with heavy casualties. Her former skipper and flotilla commander, Philip Vian, rose to the rank of Admiral and became the Commander-in-Chief of the Home Fleet before he retired in 1952.

In 1988, a little over 47 years after the *Bismarck* was sunk, the same underwater research team that had found the wreck of the Titanic in 1985, undertook an expedition to find the *Bismarck*. This team was headed by Dr. Robert D Ballard of the Woods Hole Oceanographic Institute on Cape Cod and was sponsored by the National Geographic Society. They were initially unsuccessful, but on the team's second attempt a year later, one of the cameras on the underwater robot vehicle *Argo* began to pick up debris on the ocean floor in the vicinity of the *Bismarck*'s last reported position.

Epilogue

After searching the area for the next few days, the team finally came across the wreck of the *Bismarck* on the morning of 9 June 1989, at a depth of little over 15,000ft. Dr Ballard's team spent another couple of days making detailed observations of the main part of the wreckage and combing the surrounding area for other debris. Photographs were taken and compared against earlier pictures of the ship to identify the secondary objects discovered and to assess the damage she had sustained. With their allotted time running out, the team sailed back to their home port of Cadiz, Spain

The visual observations made by Dr Ballard and his team, together with the photographic evidence, revealed the true extent of the damage inflicted on the *Bismarck* in her last battle with the Royal Navy. Much of her superstructure was blown away, and scores of hits could be seen on her hull, conning tower, and two upper decks. Her four 15in-gun turrets, which fell out of her hull when she capsized, landed some distance away from the main part of the ship. The end of her stern section, undoubtedly weakened by the torpedo hit that crippled her, had broken off when the *Bismarck* hit the ocean floor and landed nearby.

Thus ended the story of the *Bismarck*, with the ship at the bottom of the Atlantic Ocean some 500 miles short of her destination on the French coast, but still providing details of what happened on that fateful day of 27 May 1941. One of the most famous sea battles in history, the *Bismarck* chase has been the subject of an excellent film, a hit song and numerous documentaries, and still holds the interest of millions of people. While this book does much to resolve the remaining questions about the battle, it will certainly not be the last word written about it.

APPENDIX A

Naval Gunnery

Gunnery was the essential factor in all naval engagements up until the middle of the twentieth century. After that time, surface-to-surface missiles had been developed to the point that naval gunnery was made obsolete. The encounter between the British and German forces in the North Atlantic in May 1941 was one of the last times that gunnery played a critical role in the outcome of a naval battle. To better appreciate what happened during that battle, an understanding some basic principles of naval gunnery is useful. Rather than clutter the text and interrupt the storyline of the battle, the essential elements of naval gunnery are presented in this appendix.

As one can imagine, it was extremely difficult to hit a moving target at extreme ranges, especially when the firing platform was itself moving. The aim therefore was not to hit the place where the target was seen through the gunsights of the firing ship, but rather where the target would be when the shells eventually landed. With a projectile flight-time of about a minute at 30,000 yards, a target steaming at 30 knots would have progressed 1000 yards before the shells reached their destination. Since the ships involved in this engagement were less than 300 yards long and 40 yards wide, they did not present easy targets to hit at that range.

Once an enemy ship was spotted, it had to be tracked by taking its bearing and estimated range at periodic intervals until its course and speed had been established. This required careful plotting of the attacking ship's course and speed as well as that of the enemy ship to determine the relative position of each ship at the time that those measurements were taken. If the enemy ship maintained direction and speed, it was possible to work out a gunnery solution to the problem, but there were factors that limited the effectiveness of gunfire based on such solutions. If the enemy ship took evasive action, it then became a guessing game as to which direction the enemy ship would turn to avoid the projectiles fired by the attacking ship and this made the problem more difficult.

One of the most important factors in effective naval gunfire was accurately determining the range to the target. By 1941, the optical rangefinder used for naval gunnery had reached its ultimate state of development which had begun just before the turn of the century. It would become obsolete within a couple of years by the development of radar technology to the level where it could outperform the optical rangefinder, especially at longer ranges. The optical rangefinder depended on the length of its base to determine the range to a distant object by triangulation. As the ranges increased, the angle being measured became so small that minor changes represented large differences in range. For example, at 30,000 yards, an error of only two hundredths of a degree (0.02°) on the 30-ft rangefinder of the *Hood* would translate into an error of 1000 yards in the range taken.

Anyone familiar with a rangefinder camera can fully appreciate the limitations of an optical rangefinder. At distances up to one or two yards, you could measure the distance to an object within an inch or so. As ranges increased, you could measure distances only up to the nearest foot. Between 30 and 50ft, you could break that down into 5ft increments, and between 50 and 100ft, you might be able to guess at 10-ft intervals. The last ⅛in on the scale took you from 100ft to infinity. That was sufficient for picture taking, but not for range-finding beyond 50ft. Of course, with a camera, one is dealing with a rangefinder base of only a couple of inches compared with 30 to 50ft for naval rangefinders, but the principle is the same. In fact, the ability to accurately determine ranges with an optical rangefinder decreases with the square of the distance.

The longest base achieved for naval rangefinders was 15m (nearly 50ft) on the Japanese battleship *Yamato*. By contrast, the *Bismarck* carried 10m (33ft), the *Hood* and *Prince of Wales* 30ft, and the *Prinz Eugen* 7m (23ft) rangefinders. The quadruple turrets of the *Prince of Wales* were equipped with rangefinders having a base of just over 40ft, but due to their low placement, they could not be

Appendix A

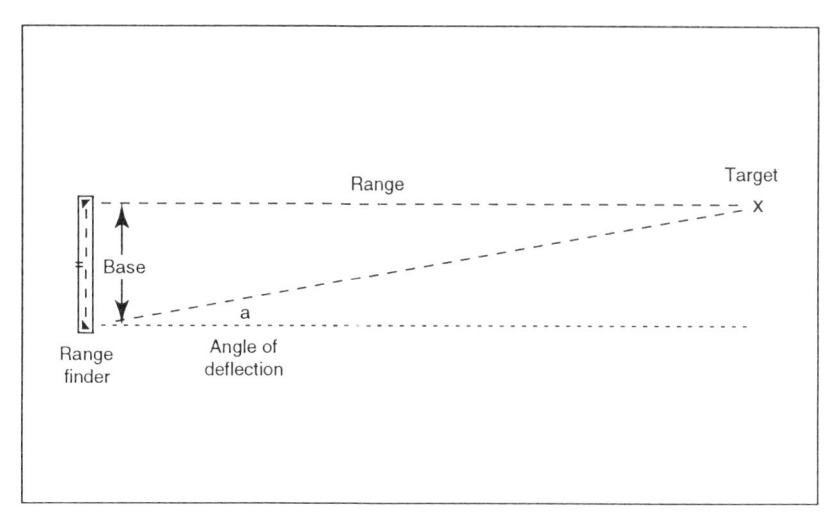

A-1 Principle of operation of an optical rangefinder.

used at long ranges. In addition to the somewhat wider base of the rangefinders on the *Bismarck* compared with those on her British counterparts, the superior Zeiss optics on the German devices gave her a slight advantage in range determination, especially in conditions of poor visibility.

There were two types of optical rangefinders in use at the time, the coincidence (or split-image) and the stereoscopic. The first type was favoured by the British primarily for its simplicity. One of the optical elements (located at one end of the rangefinder housing) was used to isolate the top half of the image, and the other (located at the opposite end), the bottom half. Looking through a single eyepiece, the observer would turn a knob to change the angle of orientation between the two optical elements until both halves were lined up to form a coincided image. If the observer was looking at a ship's mast in the distance, all he had to do was bring the top of the mast in vertical alignment with the bottom half of the mast and read off the range calibrated from the relative position of the optical elements.

The Germans preferred the stereoscopic-type rangefinder which produced a sharp, three-dimensional image when the optical elements were exactly focussed on the target. It required two eyepieces to achieve the stereoscopic effect, and under certain conditions, it could be used by experienced operators to determine the range more accurately. It was much more complex than the coincidence rangefinder, and it required frequent calibration. Most naval stereoscopic rangefinders had a built-in collimation system that reduced the need for more frequent calibration. Due to their nature and complexity, stereoscopic rangefinders needed a higher level of skill to operate, and this in turn led to greater training requirements.

Another important factor in naval gunnery was gun-laying. This required the training of the guns so as to be able to hit the target at the bearing and range predetermined from optical observation and ranging. When the bearing of the target had been determined, the gun turrets were traversed towards the target. Each twin 15-inch gun turret weighed 900 tons on the *Hood* and 1100 tons on the *Bismarck*. The quadruple 14-inch gun turrets on the *Prince of Wales* weighed nearly 1600 tons each. These massive turrets resting on roller bearings were rotated by electric or hydraulic motors until they reached the appropriate azimuth reading corresponding to the projected bearing of the target.

Of course, the gun turrets could not be directed toward the target with the same degree of precision as an optical instrument, as there was always some slack between the turret ring gear and the gear on the drive motor. It was difficult to bring the turret to a stop precisely at the prescribed azimuth, and while it was possible to make small adjustments, time usually did not permit many corrections to achieve the optimum positioning of the turret before firing. As a result, guns could not be laid to an accuracy much greater than one third of a degree (20 minutes) in azimuth.

Then there was the problem of synchronising the rotation of all three or four turrets on the ship to the same azimuth at the same time. Even slight variations in the positioning of those turrets in relation to each other could add to the margin of error for gunnery. However, parallax caused by the separation of the turrets in distance and height was not a significant problem at long ranges. For example, a separation of 150 yards between the foremost turret and the rearmost turret on a ship approximates to the level of lateral

Appendix A

dispersion of a salvo at 15,000 yards. At shorter ranges, it would be advantageous to aim each turret separately to converge fire on the centre of the target.

A similar problem existed with respect to elevation. The guns in each turret had to be elevated until they reached the predetermined angle to achieve the required range. These guns, weighing 100 tons apiece, were elevated through an arc of up to 30° or more by electric or hydraulic motors which had the same limitations as those of the traversing system. Slack in the gear train and the difficulty in bringing the elevated mass to a halt at precisely the prescribed angle affected the accuracy of gun-laying in the vertical plane to the same degree as in the horizontal plane.

The accuracy achieved by the guns on a ship was dependent on the elevation of the gun tubes in relation to a fixed line of reference, *ie*, sea level. The movement of the ship, especially its rolling action, greatly affected the actual vertical angle at which the guns were pointed. In the old days of the sailing navy, the crew had to watch the inclinometer (an instrument that used a freely-suspended weight moving in an arc along a fixed scale to measure the roll of the ship) and wait until the ship reached the horizontal before they could fire their guns. Advancements in technology later allowed for the continuous compensation of a ship's roll and pitch in setting the elevation of the guns.

The cumulative effect of these limitations on precisely accurate gunlaying was the dispersion of the rounds in a salvo within an angle of about 0.5 per cent. This translated to a spread of about 1 per cent of the range. For example, if the range to the target was 20,000 yards, there would be a spread of about 200 yards when the shells fired in that salvo reached the target. In the vertical plane, this dispersion was circular, similar to the shot pattern from a shotgun. In the horizontal plane, this dispersion was elliptical. The lateral dispersion remained 200 yards, but the longitudinal dispersion was dependent on the impact angle of those shots, as explained below.

A further factor affecting accuracy involved the shell and its trajectory to the target. The theoretical range and time of flight of a projectile could be easily calculated by a simple formula involving the angle of gun elevation and the muzzle velocity of the projectile.

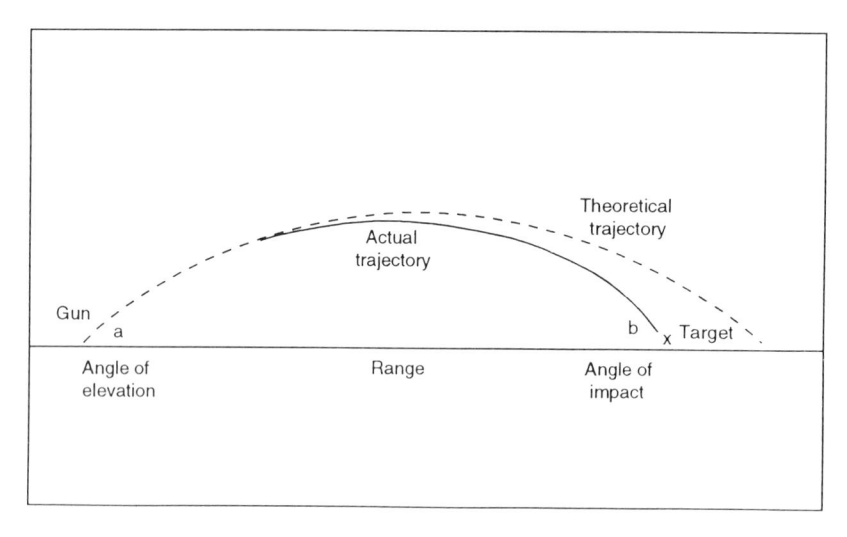

A-2 Comparison of actual trajectory with theoretical trajectory.

These calculations, however, were based on the projectile travelling in a perfect vacuum. In actual practice, it had to pass through various levels of air with different densities, and this had a profound effect on the ballistics of that projectile. At 30,000 yards and over, air resistance reduced the range of a projectile by 60–80 per cent, depending upon the size and shape of the shell and other variables.

This air resistance also affected the angle at which the projectile returned to the surface at the end of its flight. The relation of the impact angle to the elevation angle was almost a linear function. The impact angle ranged from about 30 to 50 per cent greater than the elevation angle depending on the range and type of gun used. Assuming an impact angle of 30° in the example cited above, the linear dispersion of the shells in the salvo would be about 400 yards (200 yards/sin 30°). The area represented by this shot pattern is elliptical and measures about 64,000 square yards. At increased ranges, the elliptical pattern of fall would become wider as the range increased, but the length of the pattern would not increase proportionally since the strike angle would become steeper with increased gun elevations. Conversely, at shorter ranges, the pattern of fall would become narrower and proportionally longer.

Appendix A

The objective in naval gunnery was to lay the pattern of fall directly over the target with as many shots falling beyond the target as in front of it, 'straddling'. At moderate ranges, the chances of getting a hit with a straddle were very good. Since the actual ballistic characteristics of a projectile did not follow a simple formula, gun tables for each type of gun had to be developed, based on extensive test data, which considered the type of projectile (armour-piercing or high-explosive) and various propellant charges. Gunners were provided with these to guide them in setting the proper elevation of the guns to achieve the desired range.

There were yet further problems that could affect the accuracy of naval gunnery. Barrel wear could cause a gradual drop in the trajectory of a projectile as the wear progressed and the gun tubes tended to droop slightly after they had been fired several times and heated up, and this could affect the range achieved by the gun. Differences in ambient temperature could also affect the ballistics of the gun, both as to firing pressures and the effect of temperature on the density of the air through which the projectile had to pass. Humidity could affect the propellant and cause differences in the muzzle velocity and the trajectory of a projectile. There was also the wind factor which could be sufficient to deflect the projectile from its original bearing.

In the final analysis, perhaps the most important factor in naval gunnery was the gunnery officer himself. His experience and skill could do much to overcome some of the technical limitations of the equipment involved. The ability of the gunnery officer to properly identify the target, judge its course and speed, anticipate moves by the enemy commander, calculate the firing solution, co-ordinate with his ship's commander, and fire at the appropriate time became an art as well as a science. His skill in accurately and promptly making the necessary corrections after each fall of shot was of paramount importance to assure the destruction of the enemy and for self preservation. The First Gunnery Officer of the *Bismarck*, Commander Adalbert Schneider, was awarded the Knight's Cross for his skill in sinking the *Hood* before he went down with his ship.

In view of the variables involved, the fall of shot from the first salvo was usually a clean miss. The gunnery officer had to then

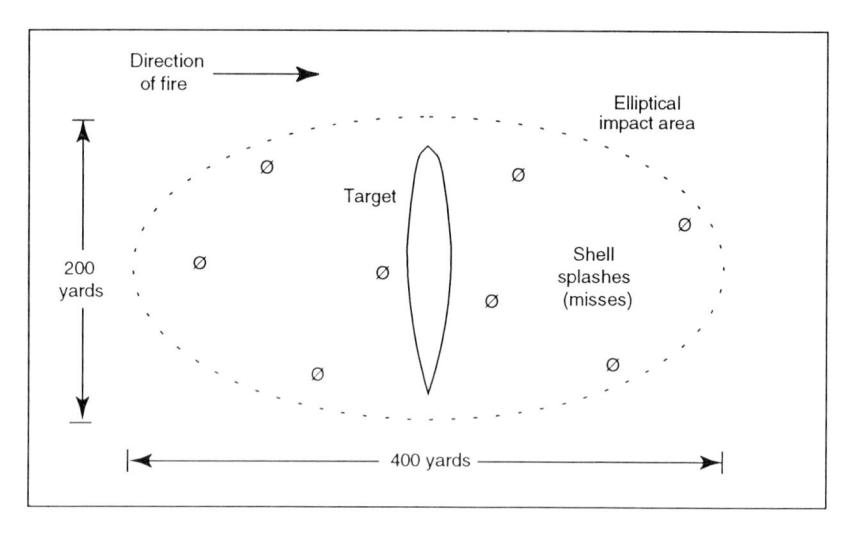

A-3 Plan view of hypothetical impact area for an eight-round salvo at 20,000 yards.

make accurate and prompt corrections based on each fall of shot to ensure that the next salvo fell closer to the target. The objective of any gunnery officer, recognising the uncertainty of achieving a hit at long ranges, was at least to straddle the target. If enough straddles were achieved, eventually the odds would result in a hit, and as the range droppped, the probability of achieving a hit increased as the range determination became more accurate and the size of the shot pattern contracted.

The area of the target was less than 8000 square yards (or roughly the area of an ellipse corresponding to the length and beam of the ship), so the probability of hitting it at 30,000 yards was very remote. At 25,000 yards, the odds of scoring a hit became reasonable, and at 20,000 yards, the chances of a hit were favourable. At 15,000 yards or less, a hit from every salvo was a virtual certainty. At ranges between 20,000 and 30,000 yards, a perfect straddle had about a 50 per cent chance of scoring a hit, so the real problem was getting the correct range to within 200 yards or so. A skilled gunnery officer would split his second and succeeding salvoes into two or more groups that would bracket the target until he had determined the range with a high degree of accuracy. Then he would fire several full salvoes in rapid succession for

Appendix A

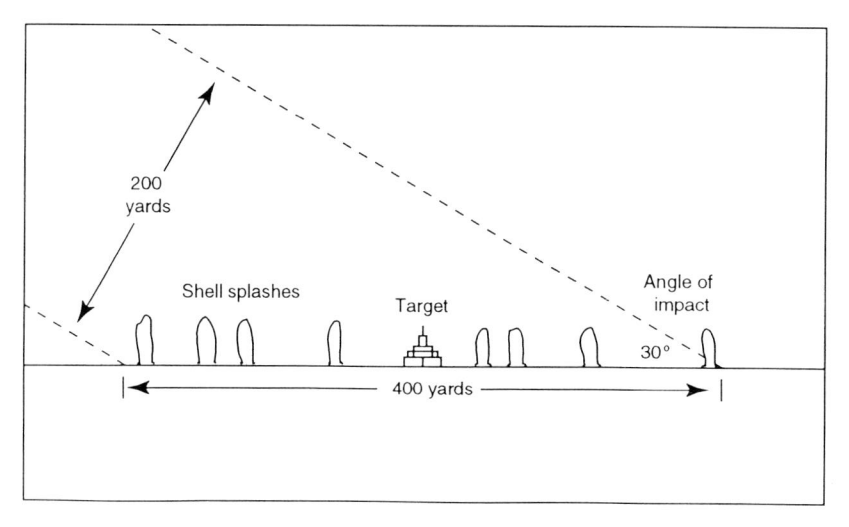

A-4 Profile view of hypothetical impact area for an eight-round salvo at 20,000 yards.

effect. He would then repeat the process until the issue was resolved.

From a defensive point of view, the objective was to position the ship outside the pattern of fall of enemy shells. This was achieved by manoeuvring the ship away from the area where the next salvo was expected to fall based on the location of the previous salvo. A trick learned by many naval commanders was to steer in the direction of the last fall of shot with the expectation that the enemy gunners would be making corrections that would put the next salvo in a different area.

The next best thing to do was to orient the ship so that it had the least probability of being hit within the pattern of the fall of shot. One means was to orient the ship directly toward the enemy so that any error in deflection (*ie*, horizontal aiming of the guns) would cause the enemy to completely miss the target. This of course was very risky since it was possible that the enemy could score multiple hits if he were very accurate in azimuth and laid a string of projectiles directly in line with the target ship.

Another means was to orient the ship perpendicular to the enemy's line of sight so that the elongated pattern of shot fall might result in all of the shells either over- or undershooting the target.

This would also allow the commander to use all of his broadside armament against the enemy. Probably the worst thing to do was to orient the ship diagonally in front of the enemy which increased the chance of a hit from one of his salvoes, the position which the *Hood* unfortunately found herself on 24 May 1941.

APPENDIX B

Bibliography

Ballard, Robert D, *The Discovery of the Bismarck* (New York 1990).
Bekker, Cajus (ed), *Die Versunkene Flotte* (Hamburg 1961).
Bekker, Cajus, *Hitler's Naval War* (New York 1974).
Breyer, Siegfried, and Koop, Gerhard, *The German Navy at War 1935–1945, Volume 1: The Battleships* (Chester, Penn. 1989).
Elfrath, Ulrich, and Herzog, Bodo, *The Battleship Bismarck* (Chester, Penn. 1989).
Forester, C S, *The Last Nine Days of the Bismarck* (Boston, Mass. 1958).
Garzke, William H, Jr, and Dulin, Robert O, Jr, *Battleships: Allied Battleships in World War II* (Annapolis 1980).
Garzke, William H, Jr, and Dulin, Robert O, Jr, *Battleships: Axis and Neutral Battleships in World War II* (Annapolis 1985).
Grenfell, Russell, *The Bismarck Episode* (New York 1962).
Grove, Eric, '*Hood*'s Achilles' Heel', *Naval History Magazine*, Vol 7, No 2 (1993).
Hailey, Foster, and Lancelot, Milton, *Clear for Action* (New York 1964).
Hoyt, Edwin P, *Sunk by the Bismarck* (New York 1980).
Humble, Richard, *Hitler's High Seas Fleet* (New York 1971).
Hughes, Terry, and Costello, *The Battle of the Atlantic* (New York 1977).
Kemp, Paul J, *Bismarck and Hood* (London 1991).
Kemp, Peter K (ed), *History of the Royal Navy* (New York 1969).
Kennedy, Ludovic, *Pursuit* (New York 1974).
Müllenheim-Rechberg, Baron Burkard von, *Battleship Bismarck* (Annapolis 1980).
Preston, Anthony, foreword to *Jane's Fighting Ships of World War II* (New York 1989).
Raven, Alan, and Roberts, John, *British Battleships of World War Two* (Annapolis and London 1976).

Raven, Alan, and Roberts, John, *British Cruisers of World War Two* (London 1980).

Rimell, Ray, *Swordfish* (Linewrights Ltd 1988).

Roberts, John, *The Battlecruiser Hood* (Annapolis 1982).

Robertson, R G , 'HMS Hood', *Warships in Profile*, Volume 2 (New York 1973).

Roskill, S W, *White Ensign* (Annapolis 1960).

Ruge, Friedrich, *Der Seekrieg* (Annapolis 1957).

Schmalenbach, Paul, 'Kriegsmarine Bismarck', *Warships in Profile* Volume 2 (New York 1973).

Schmalenbach, Paul, 'Kriegsmarine Prinz *Eugen*' *Warships in Profile* Volume 1 (New York 1972).

Schmalenbach, Paul S, and Wise, James E, Jr, '*Prinz Eugen* Album', *US Naval Institute Proceedings*.

Schofield, B B , *The Loss of the Bismarck* (Annapolis 1972).

Shirer, William L, *The Sinking of the Bismarck* (New York 1962).

Showell, Jak P Mallmann, *The German Navy in World War Two* (Annapolis 1979).

Statz, Josef, 'I Escaped from the *Bismarck*', *Naval History Magazine* Vol 9, No 1 (1995).

Stephen, Martin, *Sea Battles in Close-up: World War 2* (Annapolis 1988).

Taylor, Theodore, *HMS Hood vs Bismarck* (New York 1982).

Van der Vat, Dan, *The Atlantic Campaign* (New York 1988).

Von der Porten, Edward P, *The German Navy in World War II* (New York 1969).

Warner, Oliver, *Great Sea Battles* (London/New York 1968).

Whitley, M J, *German Cruisers of World War Two* (Annapolis 1985).

INDEX

Abbreviations
Aus = Austro-Hungarian; Br = British; Fr = French; Ger = German; HMAS = His Majesty's Australian Ship; HMNZS = His Majesty's New Zealand Ship; HMS = His Majesty's Ship; It = Italian; Jpn = Japanese; Pol = Polish; RAF = Royal Air Force; RN = Royal Navy; Rus = Russian; Sp = Spanish; Sw = Swedish; Trk = Turkish; US = United States of America; USS = United States Ship

Achilles, HMNZS 40
Admiral Graf Spee (Ger) 39, 133, 144, 147
Admiral Hipper (Ger) 45, 62, 64
Admiral Scheer (Ger) *38*, 39
Agincourt, HMS 13
Ajax, HMS 40
Akagi (Jpn) 29
Altmark (Ger) 144-146
Arado-196 float-plane (Ger) 149
Anson, HMS (1916) 19
Anson, HMS (1937) 32, 163
Arctic Circle 56, 57, 66
Arethusa, HMS 23, 66
Argo (US) 170
Ark Royal, HMS, 23, 24, 120
    attack on *Bismarck* 132-143
    loss of 169, *169*, 170
Aurora, HMS 67

Baden (Ger) 14, 42
Bayern (Ger) 13, 14
Ballard, Dr. Robert D 170, 171
Beatty, Vice-Admiral Sir David 20
Bergen (Norway), 25, 51, 64-66, 68, 75, 137
Birmingham, HMS 66
Bismarck (Ger) 7, 8, 25, 30-32, 36, 37, 45, 54, 60, 62, 63, 66, 67, 71, 112-116, 161-164, 167, 169-171, 174-176, 179
    construction 42-43
    fitting-out 44
    sea trials 43
    final training 44, 47
    becomes operational 47
    en route to Norway 45-47, 50-51
    in Norway *48*, 52-55, *65*
    en route to Iceland 55, 66
    first contact 68

in Denmark Strait 68-75
first battle 76-116, *92*, *94*, *104*, *106*, *107*, *108*, *109*
damage 111, 117, 131, 137
fuel situation 56, 113, 117, 131, 137
after the battle 117-127, *118*, *121*, *123*
escape 127-132
discovery 132
targeted 132-141, *139*
disabled 141
awaiting the end 141-143, 146-149, *148*
War Diary 147, 149
final battle 150-157, *156*, *159*
sinking of 157-160
survivors 160, 160-163
Blohm & Voss shipyard, Hamburg (Germany) 42-43, *44*
Blücher (Ger) 46
Brest (France) 25, 117, 146, 163, 164
Bretagne (Fr) 15, 23
Brinkmann, Captain Helmut, 46

Cammell-Laird, Birkenhead (England) 19, 32, 132
Canada, HMS 13
Carley raft 101, 119
Catalina flying boat 131, 132, *132*, 135
Ceylon (Sri Lanka) 166
Churchill, Winston 161, 165
Clyde, Firth of (Scotland) 67
Clyde, River (Scotland) 32
Coastal Command (RAF) 32, 64, 65, 131
Colorado USS 14
Copenhagen (Denmark) 51, 165
Corbet (Fr) 15
Cornwall, HMS 170
Cossack, HMS 144-146, 170

Dalrymple-Hamilton, Captain F H G 144, 153
Dante Alighieri (It) 15
Danzig (Gdansk) (Poland) 37
Delaware, USS 14
Denmark Strait (Iceland) 55-59, 66-69, 70-72, 131, 147
Deutschland (Ger) 39
Devonport Royal Dockyard 23
Dorsetshire, HMS 131, 153, 154, 156-162, 170

Dreadnought, HMS 9, 10, *10*, 11, 14
Duke of York, HMS 32, 163
Dunkerque (Fr) 23, 29, 30, 40
Dutch East Indies 170

Edinburgh, HMS 120
Electra, HMS 119, 166, 167, 170
Encounter, HMS 166
Enterprise, HMS 23
Erin, HMS 13
Espana (Sp) 18
Exeter, HMS 40
Express, HMS 166, 167

Faeroe Islands, 52, 55, 66, 67
Fairfield, Govan (Scotland), 19, 32
Fisher, Admiral Sir John 9, 11
Florida, USS 14
Force H (Br) 23, 67, 120, 124, 128, 132, 134, 135, 169
Force Z (Br) 166
Fourth Destroyer Flotilla (Br) 144
Furious, HMS 35
Fuso (Jpn) 18
Fyn (Denmark) 51

G3 battlecruiser design 27-28
Galatea, HMS 67
Gangut (Rus) 18
Gdansk *see* Danzig
Gdynia *see* Gotenhafen
Germania (Krupp), Kiel (Germany) 46
German Air Force *see* Luftwaffe
German Naval High Command *see* Oberkommando der Kriegsmarine
German Navy *see* Kriegsmarine
Gibraltar 23, 67, 120, 124, 166, 169, 170
Gneisenau (Ger) 29, 40, 41, *41*, 43, 45, 47, 117, 163, 164
Gotenhafen (Gdynia) (Poland) 44, 47, 50, 51, 56
Gotland (Sw) 51, 55, 57, 63, *64*
Govan (Scotland) 32
Graf Spee *see* Admiral Graf Spee
Great Belt (Denmark) 51
Greenland 7, 55, 57-59, 68, 73, 79, 80, 81
Grimstadfjord (Norway) 51, 56, 64, 65

Hamburg (Germany) 42, 43
Hercule (Fr) 19
Hermione, HMS 67
High Seas Fleet, German 37
Hindenberg, President Paul von (Ger) 40
Hitler, Adolf 40, 43, 47, 146, 161
Hjeltefjord (Norway) 51, 55, 64

Holland, Vice-Admiral Lancelot E 25, 63, 66, 69, 72, 73, 76, 78, 82-85, 87, 91-93, 95, 97, 101, 111, 119
Home Fleet, British, 21, 22, 25, 32, 52, 55, 60, 63, 66-68, 75, 79, 120, 131, 161, 170
Hood, HMS 7-9, 27, 30, 36, 43, 60, 62, 63, 71, 102, 104, 115, 120, 131, 146, 147, 150, 161-163, 170, 174, 176, 182
  construction 19-21
  sea trials *16-17*
  pre-World War II 21-23
  early World War II 23-25, *24*
  sailing against *Bismarck* 25, 36, 63, 70-75, *74*
  battle with *Bismarck* 76-101, *86*
  sinking of 97-101, *99*, 102, 104
  survivors 101, 118-119
Hood, Rear-Admiral Horace 19, 21
Howe, HMS (1916) 19
Howe, HMS (1937) 32, 163
Hvalfjord (Iceland) 58, 59, 63, 66, 119
Hyuga (Jpn) 18

Iceland 25, 36, 55-58, 63, 66, 68, 131
Illustrious, HMS 133
Imperatritsa Mariya (Rus) 18
Indefatigable, HMS 11, 20
Indomitable, HMS 166
Inflexible, HMS 15
Invincible, HMS 11, 20, *20*, 21
Isafjord (Iceland) 58
Ise (Jpn) 18

Java Sea, Battle of 170
Jean Bart (Fr) 29
Jellicoe, Admiral Sir John 20
John Brown, Clydebank (Scotland) 19, 32, 60
Jupiter, HMS 166
Jutland, Battle of 19-21

Kaga (Jpn) 29
Kalvanes (Norway) 52
Kattegat (Sweden) 51, 55, 57
Kent, HMS 59
Kenya, HMS 67
Kerr, Captain Ralph 25, 101
Kiel Canal (Germany) *38*, 43
Kiel naval base (Germany) 43, 46
King George V, HMS 80, 93, 163, 169
  construction 32
  early World War II 30, 32, *33*
  tracking the *Bismarck* 60-62, 67, 72, 101, 130, 131, 135, 144
  battle with *Bismarck* 150-157

186

Index

Kongo (Jpn) 18
Korsfjord (Norway) 51
Kriegsmarine (German Navy) 146
Kristiansand (Norway) 51
Krupp Germania *see* Germania
Kuantan (Malaya) 166, 167
Kwajalein Atoll 165

Leach, Captain John C 35, 36, 85, 86, 91, 102, 105, 106, 108, 111, 117, 118, 120, 166, 168
Leipzig (Ger) 164
Lexington, USS 28, 29
Lindermann, Captain Ernst 43, 56, 141, 143
Lion, HMS 11, 20
Littorio (It) 29
London, HMS 120
London Naval Treaty 29, 31, 32, 35, 40-42
Luftwaffe (German Air Force) 23, 50, 137, 138, 146, 147, 161, 169
Lütjens, Fleet Admiral Günther 47, *50*, 52, 55, 56, 68, 69, 73, 75, 78-82, 86-88, 94, 95, 104, 111, 113, 115, 117, 120, 125, 127, 130, 137, 141, 147, 149, 152, 161

Malaya 166, 170
Malaya, HMS 12
Manchester, HMS 66
Maori, HMS 144, 161
Mars, HMS 19
Martin, Captain Benjamin C 161
Mashona, HMS, 144, 157, 161, 162
Mers-el-Kebir (Algeria) 23
Michigan, USS 14
Montevideo (Uruguay), 40
Musashi (Jap) 35
Mutsu (Jap) 18

Nagato (Jap) 18
Naval Group West 55, 147, 149
Nelson, HMS 21, 28, 30, 131, 152
Neptune, HMS 11, 67
Nevada, USS 14
Newcastle-upon-Tyne (England) 32, 60, 162
Newfoundland (Canada) 165
New York, USS 14
Norfolk, HMS
  off Iceland *58*, 59, 66
  shadowing *Bismarck* 69, 71, 72, 79, 95, 101, 111, 118, 119, 127, 131
  battle with *Bismarck* 153, 154, 157
  fate 170
Normandie (Fr) 117

North Carolina, USS 33, 34

Oberkommando der Kriegsmarine 40, 45, 47, 68, 69, 79, 130, 134, 146, 147, 161, 164
Orion, HMS 11
Oran (Algeria) 23, 62
Orkney Islands (Scotland) 52, 67

Panzerschiff 29, 38-40, 45, 57
Pearl Harbor, US naval station (Hawaii) 166
Phillips, Admiral Sir Thomas 166, 168
Photographic Reconnaisance Unit (RAF Coastal Command) 64
Piorun (Pol) 144, 146
Pocket battleship *see* Panzerschiff
Portsmouth Royal Dockyard 22, 60
Prince of Wales, HMS 7, 8, 25, 26, *34*, 36, 60, 62, 67, 71, 113-115, 127, 130, 131, 137, 174, 176, 179
  construction 32, 35, 36
  sea trials 36
  sailing against *Bismarck* 36, 71-75
  initial battle phase 76-96
  fighting alone 102-111
  loss of 165-168, *168*
Prinz Eugen (Ger) 7, 8, 45, *46*, *46*, 47, 60-63, 71, 112, 115, 116, 127, 174
  en route to Norway 50-52
  in Norway 52-55
  en route to Iceland 55
  first contact 68
  in Denmark Strait 68-75
  battle against *Hood* 76-96
  battle against *Prince of Wales* 102-111
  escape 121-122
  fate 164-165, *165*
Provence (Fr) 23

Queen Elizabeth, HMS 11-13, 21
Queen Mary, HMS 20

Ramillies, HMS 120
rangefinders 174-176
Renown, HMS 13, 21, 80, 120, 135
Repulse, HMS 13, 21, 60, 62, 67, 80, 120, 130
  loss of 166-167
Reshadieh (Trk) 13
Resolution, HMS, 23
Revenge, HMS 120
Reydarfjord (Iceland) 59
Reykjavik (Iceland) 58
Rheinübung, Operation 45, 47, 117, 162, 163

187

Rhine Exercise, Operation *see* Rheinübung
Richelieu (Fr) 29
River Plate, Battle of the 144
Rodney, HMS 19, 21, 28, *28*, 30, 80, 120, 131, 135, 144, 168
   final battle 150-157, *155*
Rosyth Royal Dockyard (Scotland) 25, 130
Royal Air Force (RAF) 52, 64, 67, 75, 131, 166
Royal Oak, HMS 163
Royal Sovereign, HMS 13, 21, 80

Sachsenwald (Ger) 162
St. Nazaire (France) 117, 127, 130, 137
Saratoga, USS 28, 29
Scapa Flow naval base (Scotland) 23-25, 32, 34, 36, 37, 52, 60, 63, 66, 68, 79, 90, 94, 131, 161, 163
Scharnhorst (Ger) 29, 40, 41, 43, 45, 47, 117, 163, 164
Schlesien (Ger) 37
Schleswig-Holstein (Ger) 37
Schneider, Adalbert 147, 179
Seydisfjord (Iceland) 59
Sheffield, HMS, 120, *133*, 134-139, 142, 170
Shetland Islands (Scotland) 52, 59, 67
Sikh, HMS 144
Singapore naval base (Malaya) 166, 167, 170
Sixth Destroyer Squadron (Br) 162
Sjaelland (Denmark) 51
Skaggerak (Denmark) 51
Somerville, Vice-Admiral Sir James 120, 124, 135, 142
Southampton, HMS 66, 134
South Carolina, USS 14
South Dakota, USS 34
Spichern (Ger) 164
Spitfire photographic-reconnaissance aircraft, 64
Stavanger (Norway) 51, 145
Stockholm (Sweden), 51, 57, 60
Strasbourg (Fr) 23, 24, 29, 40
Suffolk, HMS
   on patrol off Iceland 59, 66, 68
   contact with *Bismarck* 68, 69, 71-73, 79, 87, 95, 118, 119, 121, 125, 127, 130, 131
   fate 170
Swan-Hunter, Wallsend-on Tyne (England), 32

Swordfish torpedo aircraft 122-124, *125*, 128, 132, 135-143, *139*, *143*, 148

Tartar, HMS 144, 157, 162
Tegetthoff (Aus) 18
Tenedos, HMS 166, 167
Tennant, Captain William G 167
Texas, USS 14
Tirpitz (Ger) 30, 32, 42, 43, 45, 47, 163
Toulon naval base (France) 24
Tovey, Admiral Sir John C 60, 61, *61*, 63, 66, 67, 72, 101, 120, 122, 128, 130, 137, 142, 144, 150, 153, 157
Trident, HMS 164
Trondheim (Norway) 56
Tsushima, Battle of 9

U-boats (Ger) 45, 125, 134, 146, 149, 161-163, 170
Unrifled Projectile Launchers 24, 90

Valiant, HMS 23
Vampire, HMAS 166, 167
Versailles, Treaty of 29, 37, 38, 40, 41
Vian, Captain Philip 144, *145*, 146, 151, 157, 170
Vickers-Armstrong, Tyne (England) 32, 36, 60, 63
Vickers, Barrow-in-Furness (England) 13, 18
Victorious, HMS 60, 62, 67, 122, 125, *125*, 130, 131, 169
Vickenes (Norway) 52
Von der Tann (Ger) 20

Wake-Walker, Admiral William Frederick 59, 69, 101, 111, 118-120, 127, 128
Walrus seaplane 102, 167
Warspite, HMS *12*
Washington, USS 33
Washington Naval Treaty 21, 22, 26-28, 31
Weissenburg (Ger) 56
Westplatte (Poland) 37
Wilhelmshaven naval shipyard (Germany) 42, 165
Woods Hole Oceanographic Institute Cape Cod (US) 170
Wyoming, USS 14

Yamashiro (Jpn) 18
Yamato (Jpn) 35

Zulu, HMS 144